MW01168821

Twenty Won

21 Female Entrepreneurs Share their Stories of Business Resilience During a Global Crisis

Curated by Kelli A. Komondor

Foreword by Renee DeMichiei Farrow

C. K. Roberts Publishing

Pittsburgh, PA

TWENTY WON: 21 FEMALE ENTREPRENEURS SHARE THEIR STORIES OF BUSINESS RESILIENCE DURING A GLOBAL CRISIS

Printed in the United States of America

Coaching by Cori Wamsley
Cover design by Karen Captline
Edited by Jim Vivirito, Aurora Corialis Publishing

ISBN: 9798726674445

Disclaimers

The advice and strategies found within this book may not be suitable for every situation. This work is sold with the understanding that neither the authors nor the publisher or those who worked on this book are held responsible for the results accrued from the advice in this book.

The information contained in this book is not intended to be a substitute for council from doctors, therapists, financial advisors, or other professionals. The reader should consult a professional to discuss a plan for addrressing their specific lives, particularly relating to symptoms that may require diagnosis or medical attention.

Advance Praise

I was immediately hooked by the profound power and impact of this book in the midst of what's happening to lives and businesses in the early months of 2021. This book is filled with inspiring stories of not only personal triumph and perseverance but also massive business success. Each woman shares how her life lessons, personal trials, and experiences set the stage for her to rise above the challenges of 2020. However, this isn't just a feel-good book! It's filled with practical tips and advice on how to handle challenges in your business and life, as well as how to strengthen your mindset and resilience to better handle the unexpected.

As an entrepreneur, reading books has been instrumental to my success over the past seven years. That's why in 2019 I decided to write and release my own bestselling book focusing on skills and strategies to elevate your beliefs and mindset for success. There are a ton of story compilation books that give only share inspiration and motivation. Every single woman in this book shares her powerful story along with specific tools, techniques, questions, and strategies.

Due to the diversity of the authors, *Twenty Won* is a practical guide to successfully navigate business challenges in any industry. Even with years of business experience, I gleaned new insights and enjoyed the new perspective on old concepts, enjoying the emotion and lessons of every contributor. Throughout the book, what resonates with me the most is how each woman followed her passion and purpose to manifest her desires and create success on her own terms.

Whether you're just starting out in business or are a seasoned veteran, you'll enjoy the empowering stories and practical strategies that are beautifully woven together. From self-care and emotion management to what you offer and how your lead, this book has you covered inside and out. *Twenty Won* will help you reconnect to your magic, passion, and purpose to help you pivot for success in any situation while staying true to YOU. Enjoy!

Stacy Raske

Bestselling Author, Podcast Host, Leadership Mentor, & Success coach
www.stacyraske.com
www.amazon.com/author/stacyraske
www.facebook.com/stacy.raske

* * *

Upon opening this book, I knew I would be inspired. However, it exceeded my expectations. As an author, radio personality, and business owner, I know we have many ups and downs as we navigate the waters to success, freedom, and happiness. But what drives us to make those decisions to take a leap and persevere no matter how high a wave comes at us?

For me, every obstacle I have faced makes me not only push harder to achieve what I desire, but also makes every step of the process less scary. Most importantly, having the support of other determined women makes all the difference in the world.

Kelli and the other twenty amazing women featured in *Twenty Won* offer not only support, but honesty in their personal stories and lessons they have learned while striving for success on their terms. Insightful, thought provoking, and entertaining, this work is a must read for any woman who is ready to seek all that life beholds, no matter what twists and turns are presented along the way.

Jess Branas

Host of Drinks with Jess Podcast
CEO of Branas Enterprises
www.dwjphl.com/drinks-with-jess-podcast-episodes.html
www.branasenterprises.com/

* * *

For more than 50 years, I've devoted my life to creating equal opportunities for women and girls. It has been incredibly rewarding work, but there's one great unspoken truth – all the opportunity in the world is worthless if no one takes advantage of it.

This book contains the stories of women who stepped up and took advantage of the opportunities available to them. And they did it, as women often do, in less than ideal situations, giving their blood, sweat, and tears to make a better world—for themselves, their families and friends, and their communities.

To paraphrase Shakespeare, "Oh brave new world that has such women in it!"

These women are leaders and role models, and their stories reflect their courage and commitment. Reading their stories showed me a wonderful vision of the future that all women and girls should know about.

Jeanne K. Clark

Director of Governmental Affairs, Allegheny County Sanitary Authority
Grassroots Organizer, Trainer, Author, and Media Consultant for Feminist, Civil Rights, LGBTQ, the Environment, and Other Social Justice Causes

* * *

Women are so resilient! Kelli Komondor assembles milestones and journeys of a group of superstars highlighting their stories of persistence, courage, and flexibility.

This anthology struck a chord and will inspire me for more: to do more, to be more grateful, to be a better friend, partner, sister, and mom. We do not stop to think about our achievements because we are busy working the "shifts" of professional responsibilities, family, and home duties, as well as finding time to give back. We continue to persevere no matter the circumstances, seldom taking time to account for the milestones we're achieving. As a fellow entrepreneur, cancer survivor, and aspiring human, each of these stories resonated with me in some way.

Twenty Won serves as a reminder to listen, to lift each other up, and to celebrate successes big and small. This is not a dress rehearsal; there are no do overs. Live each day with vigor but also schedule time for feeding your soul, appreciating those around you, and caring for the shell that embodies you to perform monumental tasks.

Tina Winner

Co-founder and Managing Partner of Winner Partners

www.winnerpartners.net/

* * *

An extremely powerful set of stories told through the eyes of 21 remarkable female entrepreneurs.

As I read through each page, I found myself hanging on to every word with baited breath, excitement, inspiration, and even elements of thought-provoking sadness. This book serves as a wonderful case study for those embarking on the development of one's leadership journey. The qualities of a true leader resonated all through this book, including compassion, gratitude, integrity, influence, respect, and yes . . . self-awareness. The stories shared by these twenty-one courageous entrepreneurs will lead to inspiration and encouragement for the next generation of business leaders and change agents to follow in their footsteps. COVID-19 may have held the world captive, but these phenomenal women, who became even more resilient in the face of adversity, decided to remain positive and steadfast. AWESOME!

Rhonda Carson Leach

Senior Program Director of The Institute for Entrepreneurial Excellence at the University of Pittsburgh

* * *

Leading from the heart is so powerful, especially during times of crisis. Reading the success stories of so many inspiring women is a validation of our inner power and a reminder of the extraordinary things we can do when we live true to ourselves.

Kim Chestney

Author of *Radical Intuition* + Founder of IntuitionLab

www.kimchestney.com

* * *

This collaboration has produced a beautiful concert of thoughtful, insightful, and inspirational content. *Twenty Won* will have a positive impact on all who understand the thinking and process behind the project. Enjoy this book!

Dorothy Andreas

Speaker, Author, Consultant
CEO of Streamline Success, Founder of The Sewickley Spa

www.streamlinesuccess.com/

* * *

Twenty Won won my heart! These high energy, passionate women teach us how to succeed in following your dreams and living your authentic self. Entrepreneurs will benefit from this treasure trove of knowledge and experience. This book is required reading for anyone contemplating starting or expanding their business. Follow these leaders, and you will be on your own path to success!

Lisa Marie Bernardo, Ph.D., M.P.H., R.N., C.E.P., C.C.E.T., 500-YT

Owner of Fitness for Body, Mind, Spirit

www.lisabernardo.com

* * *

This book is a testament to the feminine spirit of resilience, courage, adaptability, and strength. It was moving to read accounts of women who have defied the odds, stood up for what is right, and lived their lives in authentic and meaningful ways. If you are looking for a place to feel inspired, reinvigorated and encouraged, I recommend picking up *Twenty Won*. When women work together in a spirit of collaboration, we can achieve great things. This past year has taught us that what really matters is community. May we build it, may we be strengthened by it, and may we reflect back on it so we can empower the next generation of leaders. Use this book as a jumping off point to reclaim your sisterhood, and let's remember to center the most vulnerable in the spirit equity. Let's rise together.

Natalie Bencivenga

Socially Conscious Journalist and Media Personality

www.nataliebencivenga.com

* * *

How many people have thought, "Here is a solution . . ." or "My skill is more valuable than what I'm paid for it . . ." only to fade away into the day to day? Stepping out into your own venture can be tough if you are not from a family of entrepreneurs or without a mentor. However, this book is filled with stories, insights, and inspiration to take that first step and support you along the path.

Selena Schmidt

Co-founder and Principal, The Art of Democracy Executive Director, CORO Center for Civic Leadership

Table of Contents

Foreword

By Renee DeMichiei Farrow

President, Decorating Details
Professional Coach, Results With Renee Farrow

In 2005, I had the honor to come face to face with Kelli Komondor at the business journal where I started working. She later told me that she was intimidated by me, because I had won a few awards and was talked up by a manager, and she was not sure how our personalities would jive.

I am not sure how quick it was for her, but I felt I connected immediately with Kelli. She just had that warm welcoming face, smile, and fantastic persona. Our friendship grew over the years. I always want to help everyone, so I took Kelli under my wing, and that friendship led to mentoring, which bloomed into a lifelong journey. We are so much alike: animated, full of energy, networkers, connectors.

The book: how did it happen? I started taking professional coaching classes at Duquesne University in August of 2020 and needed a practice client to coach. Kelli started her business, K2 Creative, in June, so it was perfect timing. As her coach, I listened to her, asked thought-provoking questions, and allowed her to dig deep to find the answers. Through a lot of support and hard work, she grew her business and decided to make her dream of creating this book come true. Of course, she asked me to be part of it and to also write this foreword, and I was honored. Once Kelli has her task in hand, look out! She had her plan laid out, looked at her network, found who could help, enlisted authors, and went to work. This book is the result of all of that, and I'm so pleased to see this dream come to fruition.

There are so many lessons to learn in life, when it comes to business, family, relationships, clients, and especially yourself. In a later chapter, I'll share my tips for running a successful business, and I know these suggestions along with those of the other 20 women entrepreneurs will set you straight on a path toward true accomplishments.

I am so glad that, by reading on, you'll be able to understand what we endured, discover our inspiration to push toward our own dreams, and become empowered by the true stories of perseverance in this book, *Twenty Won*. After reading it, maybe you will make the decision to start or purchase a business of your own or run a nonprofit, if you aren't already on that path. It will bring you a life of true worth, value, and an "I did it" attitude. That is what this book and all the true-life stories of the contributors bring to life.

This book includes stories of challenges in life, sadness, and true loss, which will have an impact on you. Hopefully, these stories will lead you toward living your Ideal Life by being your Ideal Self. We all strive to believe that we can do or be anything—after all, we hear it from so many people who love and believe in us. But those times of challenge can make it tough, so I'm glad that the women of this book believed in themselves enough to keep reaching for their goals. I certainly believed in myself, and Kelli sure believed in herself! She had the courage and fortitude to bring this book to life—to not only get it off her bucket list, but to prove she could do it and help so many people at the same time.

I am honored that Kelli asked me to write the foreword to *Twenty Won*. I wanted to share my big takeaway of why this book is an accomplishment for not only Kelli and me, but every single one of these strong women who share their stories of perseverance. You will have the pleasure and honor to walk through their lives with them and experience all they have to offer, which could help you see that, yes, it is possible to do the impossible. I challenge you to read each story and truly live it through their eyes. Take away one learning idea, write it down, practice it, live it, and find your Ideal Self. I am proud to be part of this amazing compilation of *Twenty Won* stories. Please enjoy the journey and connect with us.

Introduction

My pap once told me my gram was "garage kept." I knew what he meant—she didn't work outside the home. She didn't have the wear and tear associated with a job or career. The closest she came to working, besides all the duties of a housewife in the '40s, '50s, and beyond, was making pierogi and stuffed cabbages at her church. And she worked at the local jewelry store around Christmas time—for the discount!

My mom started working evenings, when my sister and I were young, and eventually worked full-time once we were old enough to come home from school on our own. Prior to that she was the typical stay-at-home mom of the '70s and '80s, with a working husband, the spotless house, dinner on the table every evening, and homemade baked goods cooling on the counter—for no occasion, "just because."

In my family we evolved into being career-focused women. I wasn't raised in an atmosphere where I had a role model who taught me the lessons of work-life balance and how to be an entrepreneur. I didn't have a mom who wore sneakers with her business suit to hop on public transportation and travel into the city every day. Yet, my mom (and my dad) instilled a great work ethic in me, which I passed on to my own children.

I worked beginning at age 16, while in high school and during the two years I spent in college. Then, after getting married and having our two children, I worked part-time, then shifted to full-time once they got a bit older. I loved the responsibility. I loved challenges and deadlines, and I loved the structure of my days.

Until I didn't.

After working for everyone else (I'm including working for my family in this: cook, chauffeur, nurse . . . you get it!). I decided it was time for me to live my dream, own my time, and do things by my rules. In 2020, I became an entrepreneur and started my own business.

Many of the women in this book are first-time entrepreneurs within their families, like me. Others were born with the entrepreneurial spirit—they watched their parents, and even their grandparents, own businesses. Although we are all so different in how we started our businesses, and what our businesses are, we have a common thread: We pivoted and we persevered in 2020, and we want you to know how, in the hopes you will find the courage and support to make your dream of being an entrepreneur come true.

In the pages of this book, you'll meet women who had to type the words "cancer," "murder," "domestic violence," "miscarriage," "brain surgery," "addiction," and "postpartum depression" to tell their stories. You're probably asking what any of this has to do with how they successfully built and rebuilt their organizations during the pandemic. What does this have to do with their businesses?

The answer: Everything.

Twenty Won

You see, women define balance, and we define strength. We make things work with whatever we have available—whether it be time, money, or resources. We strive for, and often reach, excellence in the face of any challenge that is thrown our way. We find a way to "bounce-up" (I'll never say "bounce back" after I read Mj Callaway's chapter—and you won't either!) and keep moving forward.

You'll also see the words "empower," "growth," "centered," "faith," "inspiration," "intention," and "opportunities." There are lessons in every single chapter and indisputable advice—from women who have done it, women who left the "woe is me" at the door.

And speaking of, I fell into the woe-is-me trap the night the idea for this book came to me: Thanksgiving Eve, 2020. We were invited to South Carolina to spend the holiday with our nieces and to meet our great nephew for the first time. We debated for weeks, then canceled due to increased travel restrictions and increases in COVID cases in our county in Southwestern Pennsylvania, and in their county in South Carolina. *I was ANGRY.* We had all been following the rules, staying home, wearing a mask, washing our hands—doing everything right. From the looks of social media, people were just living their best lives—ignoring restrictions and acting like it was 2019, pre-pandemic. *Then, I got SAD.* Sad for the fact I wasn't going to be hosting my big Italian family on Christmas Eve, sad that I hadn't spent much real quality time with my kids and their significant others, and with my mom. Sad for the illness, the deaths, the devastation.

Then it hit me. A lot of good things happened in 2020. I started my business, and I knew other women who did too. I was involved with a nonprofit that expanded to a nationwide organization. I knew women who picked up the pieces, put their big-girl pants on, and made the changes necessary for growth and success—some with youngsters at home fighting for table space and Wi-Fi bandwidth while virtually learning! (Next to medical and essential workers, parents of school-aged kids are the true pandemic rock stars!)

The big push came from Renee Farrow, who you'll "meet" in this book. Renee has been a very dear friend, a partner in all things business and networking, a mentor, and—recently—my business coach. While taking classes at Duquesne University, she needed a few mentees to "practice" on. I jumped at the chance to work with her, to continue to pick her brain, and to be a part of her newest journey! During one of our sessions, she took me into my future. A very long story short, the trip ended with me opening a gift—to me, from me. It was a book . . . that I wrote! It was a very emotional session. I was happy with looking out five or so years and publishing a book. I figured that was reasonable. Always the "get it done now" person, she asked, "Why is this five or 10 years down the road? Why aren't you writing it NOW?"

Anyone who knows Renee knows you don't tell her "no" and you don't let grass grow under your feet when you're working with her. So, with a theme in mind, and Renee's support, I created my hit list of successful female entrepreneurs and got to work. It really didn't take much to find 20 other women willing to partake in this project. A few I've known for many, many years; a lot of them are women I know from Pittsburgh

Twenty Won

Women's Mastermind; and some were introduced to me when I announced this project. (Thankful again for my strong professional network!) What we did with the year 2020 is what made the difference and what made us **winners in 2021**— all *"twenty won" of us!*

Each of us is an open book—we are ready to help anyone at any time. I encourage you to reach out to the person(s) you resonate with the most or reach out to any of us "just because." While we are the ones supplying all the encouragement, we'd like to get some in return! Tell us what you loved about our stories, and what you didn't. Trust me when I say that none of us got where we are without difficult conversations.

The brave women in this book all have something we consider the "secret sauce" to our success; some of us have been using the recipe for years, while some of us have just recently concocted it. Like the family recipe for pierogi—handwritten by my gram and framed in my kitchen—things need tweaked from time to time. Think of it like this: An extra pinch of salt and a few more drops of water = Women with grit, but not without some tears. It's a nice combination!

We were all simmering at a nice pace until 2020 brought us to a boil and we had to decide . . .

Would we let the pot go unattended until it is empty and ignited in flames, or would we slow things down, keep a close eye on it, adjust the recipe, and keep going?

~ Kelli A. Komondor

Success

Twenty Won

Bounce-Up Fearless: When Everything Goes Wrong

Mj Callaway

Most people kicked off 2020 with goals and champagne toasts for a brand new year. I celebrated the sixth and last surgery related to the second breast-cancer diagnosis with water in my flute. Although I considered the major surgery my first win for 2020, I knew it presented several challenges:

The post-surgical limitations included "no driving or working" and a two-month recovery time, which would play havoc on my business and income.

As a single woman and entrepreneur, I didn't have a back-up plan if my company failed.

As the business owner, I was the face of the company, and I got benched.

Twenty Won

How do you keep your business afloat when everything goes wrong?

Choose Your Word, Change Your Year

Have you ever chosen a word for the year? I started this tradition when I became a single mom—one word of intention that worked for my personal and professional goals. Knowing what the beginning of 2020 would bring, I chose leverage. How could I leverage my recovery period? Using the same technique I shared in my workshops, I brainstormed, *What do I do with the time and energy I have?* This daily question kept me focused on possible solutions rather than all the crap related to my current situation. Questions shifted my brain out of a negative "what if" mindset and into a positive, action-focused attitude.

The sofa-surfing time, as I called it, became brainstorming sessions. On good days, I emailed event professionals, booked meetings for spring, and planned the launch party for my latest book, *Bounce-Up: Outpower Adversity, Boost Resilience, Rebound Higher.* When I felt less fatigued during the mid-morning, I scheduled Zoom calls with colleagues and my National Speakers Association (NSA) Pittsburgh board members. At the time, I held the co-presidency position. Little did I know those calls would benefit me a few weeks later.

Because I was working "on" the business instead of "in" the business, my calendar from March through August held client meetings and training workshops with a healthy stream of revenue, including an all-day training booked with a billion-dollar company for their annual sales meeting. For the first

4

time since the initial breast cancer prognosis in 2016 (which gave me a 20% chance of surviving if chemotherapy didn't work, and it had a 50% chance of working), my business was on track again. Blessed and excited, on March 1, 2020, I drove to my first client meeting in nine weeks.

And then . . .

Thirteen days later, as you know, our country shut down. It impacted all of us. It sucked. Within days, decision-makers canceled on-site sales training, resilience workshops, and conference speaking engagements. Maybe you were in a similar or tougher situation. Having pulled through adversity before, I knew how imperative it would be to make strategic choices.

It might not be the choice we want. We can let adversity control us and keep us down, or we can Bounce-Up™. Every setback demands a choice. Staying undecided becomes a choice. When we make an intentional choice, we're pledging to Bounce-Up in the face of adversity.

Success Bound: Choose Intention

What word can represent your year?

How can you be intentional about your choices?

What pledge can you make to yourself?

Twenty Won

Outpower the Odds

At one point in your life, you had beat the odds against adversity. Although our setbacks might be different, we conquered the disruptions. Those challenges made us more resilient and gave us an advantage as women business owners.

Ten years ago, I started over with $500 when my former spouse and his alcohol abuse jeopardized my safety. I had left a salaried sales job and taken a commission-based position with a national on-your-site builder. Crazy, right?!

Trying to understand how addiction would affect my kids and me, I joined a support group for women who had partners or an ex with addiction. One woman shared that she couldn't leave an abusive relationship because she couldn't financially care for her family with her dead-end job. I felt blessed to have the sales and marketing skills that provided my livelihood and wondered how I could help others. Soon afterward, I taught a free sales workshop to help those who wanted to develop sales skills. If they knew how to sell, they would always have a way to support their families.

Challenges can provide unforeseen opportunities, too. That workshop sparked the idea for my company, Mj Callaway Training & Development.

Success Bound: Outpower Odds

What strengths have you developed during adversity?

What do you know now that you didn't know before?

What can you teach or share with others?

Leverage Your Strengths

With my one-word year in mind, I brainstormed what I could leverage. "Time" was one. I could also leverage my "experience" as a journalist with over 2,000 consumer articles published and several non-fiction books under both my pen name, Rulnick, and legal name, Callaway. For several years, I put my blog and newsletter on the back burner. Now, there wasn't any excuse or valid reason to hold off. On April 24, 2020, with my old list, I revealed the challenges I overcame, how the Bounce-Up Story started, and what I hoped to share in my newsletter, "Bounce-Up Chronicles." Thrilled and grateful, I retained 90% of my subscribers.

The next step involved social media. As a Facebook user since my freelance writing days, I knew I needed to be more intentional to up-level my social-platform game. This free platform offered various options to build community, increase connections, and boost followers. Taking the Bounce-Up brand, I initiated the Bounce-Up Community and generated a monthly challenge. Besides creating a community, I wanted to produce 30 days of questions to use in a workbook or program. One 2020 goal was to get a two for one—meaning two ways to use one piece of content. Of course, I'd love to have four (or more) for one. Having been tagged as the queen of questions from a former general manager, this created a unique way to leverage one of my strengths while producing a future product (coming in 2021).

Success Bound: Leverage Strengths

What experience do you have that you can leverage to reach a current goal?

What connections can you leverage to support you?

What can you leverage to build a future product or service?

Hear Opportunities

Social media posts skyrocketed during the pandemic. Negative posts from friends and colleagues ran rabid in the first few weeks. The one common theme that surfaced frequently—people felt stuck. They were in limbo, not knowing what to do or how to get their mojo back. I could identify with that feeling as I was too familiar with the limbo state because of the health journey. So, I continued doing what I always did: I evaluated first.

From experience, I learned the key to overcoming that "stuck" feeling was asking, "What can I do right now?" The more posts I read, the more an idea for an online program formed. At the beginning of April, I kicked off *Bounce-Up: From Stuck to Success*—a four-week group program that took business owners and entrepreneurs through weekly strategic sessions to define where they were spinning their wheels and build momentum for revenue and success. They would get their mojo back!

The key to opportunities was to recognize how a particular topic consistently surfaced amongst my connections. One of my clients was a life coach who focused on anxiety. Anxiety became a hot topic in the media. Acting fast, we produced several infographics, marketing materials, and webinars on this timely subject and kicked off an anxiety campaign within days.

Success Bound: Seek Opportunities

Are you hearing a common struggle among friends and peers?

Do others ask you for suggestions around a specific topic?

Do people comment about a particular strength you have?

Count the Beans

Cut the fat, aka expenses. Why is it that we cut costs when we're up against a wall?

A few years ago, I met a well-known speaker at a conference. Over a late lunch, we shared our backgrounds, and he asked, "Is there anything I could do for you?"

So I asked, "What is something you learned that continues to help you?"

He then said, "**Stay lean**. You'll hear about speakers with big teams and massive budgets who must produce more business to support those teams and costs. Do you need everyone on your team? Do you need each of those expenses?"

During 2020, his "stay lean" tip haunted me and gave me a kick in the butt, too. Reviewing my expenditures, here are two of the several I decreased:

Graphic designs. I realized that Canva Pro, which I already paid for, produced branded infographics, team activities, and marketing materials. To this point, I spent hundreds each quarter on graphic-design work.

Memberships. Evaluating memberships, I had two questions:

1. How does my business benefit from this organization?
2. Who would be Play-Up™ players? (Players who are a few levels ahead of me in a similar business model.)

What did I deem necessary? Being a professional member of the National Speakers Association was crucial even at the almost $500 annual fee, and this didn't include the additional local chapter fee. The membership provided access to private groups filled with industry leaders, million-dollar speakers, and business advice 24/7.

Making "count the beans" a part of our business systems can keep more money in our accounts, especially during tough times.

Success Bound: Stay Lean

What benefit is there to the organization's membership?

Does each business expense provide a business benefit?

How can you tighten costs?

Play-Up to Where You Want to Be

"You only have to get things right a few times; 12 investment decisions in my career have made all the difference."

– Warren Buffet

Every day we could bounce one level higher to where we want to be. We can make the right investment in who we envision as our future selves to get to that place or position we want. With on-site training sessions and keynote speaking engagements canceled, virtual presentations would be critical to my business survival. Making the necessary investment in my skills and equipment would determine success.

It was time to Play-Up! When my son played high school basketball, he always went to specific courts that usually had pick-up games with University of Pittsburgh D-1 players. He wanted to Play-Up to the next level, knowing that playing with more talented players improved his skills.

Knowing video would expand my business footprint, I designed my tiny Bounce-Up studio which I would utilize for live streaming, producing videos, developing digital courses for my upcoming Bounce-Up University, and offering remote presentations, such as my Rock Your Sales Trivia program. Also, I had to delete several old YouTube Channels that didn't serve my brand and start over to get 100 subscribers for a custom URL. That task almost stopped me, but I knew I had to do it.

On top of this project, I needed to learn live streaming and video editing software. Did I say I needed to do this on a budget? Okay, it wasn't an easy feat; I tried scads of equipment colleagues suggested and returned a bunch before finding what worked for me.

Success Bound: Play-Up

What technology can you learn to increase your business footprint?

What do you need to stop doing to move to the next level?

What equipment do you need to up your game?

And one last Bounce-Up Moment . . .

As we come to the end of our time together, remember, you can do it. You can create small "wins" every day to reach your goals, grow your company, or keep your business afloat. Be fearless by making an intentional choice to control what you can control. Wherever you are today, these strategies will help you become fearless in your decisions and Bounce-Up higher and stronger than you were before.

Bio

Photo by JP Photography

Mj Callaway, motivational speaker and corporate results catalyst, is known for shifting staff attitudes and converting tactics into results. As a two-time survivor, she shares her trademarked strategy-driven techniques with organizations so that they can boost employees' resilience, maximize team results, and increase revenue.

Mj's sales experience includes being the only female sales executive to be a top-five producer of a national building company, selling three times her annual quota. As a former corporate sales trainer, Mj knows first-hand the disruptions professionals, managers, and executive teams handle daily while still having to be positive and productive.

Mj is a certified sales professional and certified virtual presenter. Her newly-released book, *Bounce-Up: Outpower Adversity, Boost Resilience, Rebound Higher* has been endorsed by the CEO of the Healthy Workforce Institute.

And a Few More Credentials

Founded Bounce-Up University, a digital program platform

Authored eight books, including two Warner Books best sellers

Sold a children's game to Disney

Twenty Won

Earned four Gold Awards from Parenting Media Association (PMA), a global company

Voted National Speakers Association (NSA) Pittsburgh Chapter Member of the Year

Served as past co-president of NSA Pittsburgh from 2018–2020

Customized Training & Consulting

All programs are customized to the organization or individual. A sampling of her programs:

How to Get Unstuck, Nail Your Numbers, Reinvent Your Sales Self

Rock Your Sales Trivia Training

Selling in a COVID World

Bounce-Up: From Stuck to Success

Bounce-Up Fearless: Take Change by the Hand

Connect with Mj

www.facebook.com/mjcallawayspeaker
www.facebook.com/BounceUpCommunity (for entrepreneurs and businesses)
www.linkedin.com/in/mjcallaway/
www.twitter.com/mjcallawayspeak
www.youtube.com/c/mjcallaway

www.instagram.com/mjcallawayspeaker/
www.amazon.com/Bounce-Up-Outpower-Adversity-Resilience-Rebound/dp/1734264993/

Clubhouse: @Mjcallaway

Contact Mj

Email: mj@mjcallaway.com

Site: www.mjcallaway.com

Grab Your Free Toolkits:

Grab Your FREE Sales Toolkit: www.bounce-up.com/salestoolkit

Grab Your FREE Resilient Workplace Toolkit: www.resilientworkplacetoolkit

Get weekly strategies:

www.mjcallaway.com/subscribe/

The Little Things That Lead to Big Success

Melanie Colusci

Although it feels like it was a thousand years ago (and just yesterday all at the same time), I felt like the year 2020 picked me up and, at times, nearly drowned me. I also felt like it freed me (but I will get to that later). As I have now had time to reflect on the year, I definitely remember being immersed in memories of my childhood growing up in an entrepreneurial family. You see, as a child I never really understood what being a business owner or entrepreneur meant. I just knew it was hard, sometimes not fun, and a lot of times stressful. All those memories of different challenges and hardships my family lived through while they were starting and growing their business easily bubbled to the surface as I was finding my way (and sometimes stumbling) through 2020.

Thinking back to those earlier days, I remember feeling the stress and pressure my parents felt in trying to "make it all work." It is a memory for me that sometimes feels too close to home. At times, when there was not quite enough to make ends meet, my parents would take some "short-term loans" of dollar bills and quarters from the kids' piggy banks. This memory scares me as I had lived this more than I would like to admit. I remember too well what a treat it was to be able to go out to eat once a month or even to go to McDonalds! Who would have thought that McDonalds was a treat?!

But mostly, as I think back, the loudest, clearest memory I have is vowing **I WOULD NEVER OWN A BUSINESS.**

Although I've said it over and over many times since then—that the life of a business owner was not for me—I wonder today if the saying is true: Do we all end up becoming our parents? Because no matter how hard I pushed it away and tried to ignore it, I could not keep it at bay. That entrepreneurial fire that had been smoldering for years, and at times was barely an ember, suddenly erupted into a huge burning desire that caught me like a forest fire burning out of control. I could no longer pretend. I was no longer content. I knew I was meant to do more. I was meant to be more.

Now, many years later, and after moving across the country, I have successfully grown multiple businesses, all of which I am still excited about. I must admit, they were not all planned. Some of these opportunities landed in my lap, and some have appeared because of the unique experience and expertise I have. However, they all have become what they are today because of the "blood, sweat, and tears" I put into them.

Professionally, I "grew up" in financial services. Don't laugh, but I got into the business because of the movie Pretty Woman. No, I did not want to be Julia Roberts! Rather I was absolutely enthralled with Richard Gere (and not why you think). I wanted to buy and sell companies like the high-powered person he portrayed. I found that storyline in the movie to be even more exciting and romantic than anything else! And the passion it stirred up in me led me to ultimately becoming a financial services professional at an investment company. Fast forward quite a few years and I now own and run a successful financial planning firm in Western Pennsylvania.

Over the years I counseled and advised many business owners not only in finance, but also, as I was beginning to realize, in so many more ways. There were many times the conversations morphed into discussions about marketing, business tracking, accountability, goal setting, and much, much more. As a result of this realization, I knew I had to help in more ways than what I was capable of through the financial planning firm. This ultimately led to creating my business coaching company. I found so often that these business owners I had been working with over the years were missing some of the critical foundational components they needed to achieve the success they desired.

I will be the first to admit, owning a financial planning firm and business coaching company was an interesting journey in 2020 at the beginning of a global pandemic. Remember that rather quick, harsh market correction? Yeah, me too. One day we are happily in our offices meeting with clients helping them plan their financial futures and organizing their businesses.

The next day we are relegated to our homes, unable to meet with clients, watching the bottom fall out of the market. I felt like the wind had been knocked out of me and I was carrying the weight of the world on my shoulders. I was concerned for the world, I was worried about my clients, I was terrified for my staff, and I was almost paralyzed with fear of the unknown.

What was going to happen?

Would we make it through?

Would I have to lay anyone off?

Could I still pay my bills and support my family?

What about my friends? What about my family?

So many questions and so many unknowns.

I know there were a few nights when I sat in the dark, hidden away from everyone else, and cried. Like full on ugly cry . . . cried until I could not breathe. How was I going to survive this? Failure is not a word in my vocabulary, and I could see it lurking in the corner of that dark room ready to envelop me and snuff out my fire. I had worked so hard and sacrificed so much to get to where I was, and I was feeling it slip through my fingers.

It took probably a month for that initial shock and despair to subside. As it did and I was able to gain some semblance of sanity and clarity, I realized it was time to dig in. It was time to dust myself off and pick myself up. Now more than ever it was time to practice what I had been teaching to so many other business owners.

Get back to the basics.

As my businesses had grown over the years, they seemed to become more complicated. Now, in looking back, 2020 was a silver lining as it forced me to re-evaluate and only focus on those core critical components for success. I believe there are four pillars that every business owner or entrepreneur should master. In doing this, you will be able to weather any storm. You will be able to make it through even the most difficult of times. I want to share those with you now, so let's dig in!

#1 Connect with Your Mission and Vision Statements

Why are you doing what you do? Where do you see yourself a year or three years from now? When you close your eyes do you see, feel, and hear your business in the future? When I close my eyes, I can see the furniture in the lobby, I can hear the sounds in the office, and it truly tingles right down to my toes. I challenge you to really think about this. If you do not connect on this deep of a level with your why and where you envision yourself being in the future, what is going to keep you moving forward when times are tough?

#2 Create a Repeatable Client Experience

What experience are you creating for your clients or associates? Even more importantly, can you repeat it? These experiences you create can be either positive or negative. In achieving your vision, it is critical to think about what experience you are giving your clients, staff, and team. This experience should be consistent and repeatable not only with your clients but with everyone you work with. Creating and having systems in place in your business helps you gain confidence, saves time, and makes it significantly easier when it is time to expand. In addition, it creates a feeling of dependability and security for those people that are important to your business.

#3 Have Written Goals

Are your business goals, marketing plan, and systems/processes written? When was the last time you reviewed them? Do not let your goals and plans collect dust at the bottom of your desk drawer. You will have the highest probability of accomplishing those goals if you look at and review them regularly. And tell people about them! Do not hide them away like some dark, dirty secret. The more you think about, talk about, and write about your goals, the more you will ultimately accomplish. It is so easy to get caught up in the day-to-day of life and our businesses that we risk losing track of the big picture and our roadmap to get there. Make sure you carve out time for reviewing, tracking, and implementing your goals.

#4 Your Network of Support

I made a fair number of mistakes in the creation and growth of my companies. I often felt like I was on an island and did not know what to do or where to turn. I realized how important it was to have a great network of support—to find your "tribe," so to speak. The right network of friends, mentors, and coaches can make a huge difference when it comes to accomplishing all the big and little things that can add up to great successes.

Several years ago, I was in a business partnership with a person, and it did not work out. This professional "divorce" was NOT pretty. It was so hard at times I considered quitting everything altogether. I genuinely believe it was my network of support that "saved" me. It was my amazing husband, family, friends, and other resilient, talented business owners that got me through. Had I given in to that attitude of giving up, I would not have been able to help so many more people later and experience those things that have shaped me into an even better business owner, coach, and mentor!

I know just as well as anyone that life can get in the way. Who would have predicted we would have a global pandemic that would pretty much shut down the world?! When events happen, or things pop up that distract us, it can be so easy getting caught up in putting out fires and taking care of the day to day. But it is vital that we spend time not just working in our business but also working on them.

My desire and deep belief in my vision helped me get out of bed when I least felt like it. My goals helped me stay focused on the right things for my business. The systems and processes we spent many hours creating helped reduce the pressure I felt when I knew things needed to be done but I did not want to think about it. And my network of support helped lift me up and put one foot in front of the other when I felt like quitting and wasn't sure how I was going to continue on.

Launching, growing, and maintaining a business can be as rewarding as it is challenging IF you have the right foundation in place. If you have not already, take the time to incorporate these pillars into your business, and you will soar to the next level. You do not have to do all of these at once . . . Pick one, but start today!

Believe me, I know the pressure we can put on ourselves. I can do that with the best of them. Next time you feel that pressure, I hope you will remind yourself that you do not have to accomplish something really big to be great, just little things consistently. AND, you do not have to do it alone. I promise, you can reach your goals more quickly and with less stress! You can enjoy your journey and one day, sooner or later, use your own success story to help empower and inspire others.

Bio

Photo by Lucia Cintra

Melanie Colusci is an award-winning business owner, coach, and author. She started From Start-Up to Success® to provide the expert guidance and support business owners need to start, scale, and love their businesses.

In 2008, she moved to Pittsburgh, Pa., from Bozeman, Mont., and launched Bridger Financial Group® which she still owns today. Melanie has won numerous national and local financial industry awards and has been featured in *The Wall Street Journal*, *Forbes' Wealth Managers Black Book*, and *Pittsburgh Magazine*.

An educator at heart, Melanie has authored two books: *From Start-Up to Success: Navigating the Journey to Becoming (and Staying) a Successful Entrepreneur* and *From Advisor to C.E.O. – How to Move Past Survival and Succeed with your Financial Services Business*. These books are a testament to her devotion to helping women elevate their entrepreneurial journeys. Keeping with her skill and love for helping women entrepreneurs, Melanie facilitates Pittsburgh Women's Mastermind®, an entrepreneur group for women who are committed to growing their businesses and helping other women do the same.

While passionate about her work, ask her anything about her cats, family, camping, swimming, or gardening; she will talk your ear off!

Connect with Melanie

www.fromstartuptosuccess.com

Facebook Group: www.facebook.com/fromstartuptosuccess

Instagram: @melanie.colusci_businesscoach

Pinterest: www.pinterest.com/fromstartuptosuccess

Books: www.amazon.com/Melanie-Colusci/e/B08FRPP9MM?

Laying the Foundation for Business Success Without Knowing It

Jennifer Lyker

My 2020 story is not much different than that of most parents with school-age kids. It's not particularly dramatic or unique, and I have a whole list of things to be incredibly thankful for. But I experienced challenging days, weeks that have stretched on endlessly, and moments when the overwhelm hit HARD and I felt like there was no way I could tackle everything on my plate.

But I always managed it somehow, and I ended up having an abundantly successful year in my website design business. Revenue jumped 36% compared to 2019, and I hit the magic six-figure revenue milestone for the first time! I met new clients with interesting projects and business challenges, and I partnered again with past clients to make big changes to their websites. I even hired my first team member, an assistant to help me with the day-to-day admin tasks.

I don't have a singular, magical answer about why I was able to thrive in the midst of so much uncertainty. But there are definitely a few things that brought me to a place where I could be resilient, both professionally and personally. So even if my Running a Business with Kids at Home during a pandemic story isn't movie-worthy, it's hopefully inspiring and can offer a contrast to the hard stuff we've all experienced.

In August of 2019, I sent all three of my kids to school all day for the first time. After more than a decade of building my website design business during nap times and in between school pick-ups, often with a sticky-handed toddler pawing at me, I was FINALLY going to have a full five-day work week, all to myself. I was elated!

But let's back up a bit to how I got there in the first place . . .

I started building websites back in college as a hobby, and I taught myself HTML and how to use Photoshop. After graduating with a biology degree and working for a few years in a cancer research laboratory, I knew in my gut that it wasn't a long-term fit for me. When I finally grew tired of my long daily commute and laughable salary that barely covered rent and student loans, I decided to try designing websites for money.

For the first few years, it was a side-hustle on evenings and weekends after my "real" job was over and my husband was in graduate school. I found clients through newspaper ads (it was 2004!), Google searches, and referrals from friends and family. I made a ton of mistakes, but I was being paid to create websites, which delighted me. After a couple of years, my client base was strong enough that I felt ready to take the scary leap: I quit my full-time job and was officially a website designer!

A week later I discovered I was pregnant with our first child, so the timing felt perfect.

Juggling clients and babies meant learning how to be a mom and a business owner at the same time. Mostly I didn't have a plan, but I loved the work I was doing. I made decent money considering all that was on my plate, but when I was looking ahead at the day when I would have kids in school full-time, I wanted to make sure I was doing things right.

So, in 2018, I started working with a business coach to help me fix some things in my business in preparation for the day when all the kids would be in school. Because I fell into owning a business accidentally, I had a list of things I knew I needed to change if I truly wanted to make my business stronger and more successful.

Back to the fall of 2019, when things were aligning perfectly: my hard work of the previous year with my coach was all starting to work! I was landing clients easily, typically booking projects a few months out, projects were running more smoothly, and now I was going to have a "normal" work schedule!

And I did—for about 6 months.

On March 13, 2020, I watched as the news hit fast and furious. Schools all around us were announcing closures for at least 2 weeks because of the sudden rise in . . . *what was it called? Coronavirus? COVID-something? Wait . . . DISNEY WORLD is closed?* It was all incredibly surreal.

Before the bus brought my kids home that afternoon, I mentally prepared myself: a few weeks, juggling kids while working at home. I've done this before! It will be fine! Their dad will be here too! It's just a couple of weeks.

Two weeks turned into two months, and suddenly it was summer. We kept trying to deny it, but the truth was unavoidable: the new school year was not going to be normal. Ultimately, we decided that cyber school made the most sense for us because we wanted to have even a tiny bit of control over what was coming. With both of us at home, we felt like it could work, and nothing needed to be permanent.

With that decision made, we switched our focus to how on earth we were going to manage juggling work while helping the kids through school each day. My husband is in meetings constantly, so we knew I would be leading things and he'd be the backup. My project calendar was filled until the end of summer, so I pushed back new project bookings until October so I could give myself a little bit of breathing room while we adjusted to our new routines. And from there, I would just . . . figure it out.

Twenty Won

The first day of school arrived, and my dining room was turned into a classroom with folders, a new cabinet filled with school supplies, a printer, laptops, workbooks, and bins full of things that the cyber school sent us. Then we dove in!

Back in the spring and summer, I had so many questions about how this would all affect my business. Would people stop spending money on websites when there was so much instability? Could I keep my own creative and productive energies going? It was difficult to envision a good year for website work, even a passable year, let alone a year in which I met the financial milestones I did.

When I take a moment to reflect, I can identify a few things that helped me build a business that could withstand a bumpy road—maybe not fully "crisis-proof" but at least able to take a few hits and keep going!

Relationships & Diversity

Most of my work comes from referrals. I don't pay for advertising, and I don't give much thought to my website's ranking on Google. Happy clients tell their colleagues, and friends and family tag me in Facebook posts regularly when someone asks for web designer recommendations. Business mixes with personal and, yes, sometimes it can get a little tricky, but overall, it has been such a gift! I've created relationships with my clients that have lasted a decade or more, and those relationships have led to new ones, because happy clients? THEY TALK!

With such confidence in my referral network, I didn't worry much about finding clients through 2020. That took at least one source of stress off my shoulders so I could focus on everything else that needed my attention, like teaching 2nd-grade spelling or helping with algebra.

Creating relationships with other business owners is also a high priority for me. In the past few years, I started attending monthly lunches and meetings with a couple of local networking groups. Through those groups, I have made connections that go beyond the transactional business-card exchange. They've turned into friendships and have been a place to turn not just for potential work, but advice and encouragement, which I leaned on more than a few times this past year!

Perhaps it goes without saying, but I absolutely could not have done the things I did in 2020 without my husband. He co-parented and co-taught the kids with me while juggling his own work responsibilities, and he has kept me laughing through all the ridiculousness. He has also made sure I get space and quiet when I really need it, whether it's for work or just to stare at Netflix for a while!

Clear Services & Solid Systems

One of the best things that came out of working with a business coach was figuring out exactly what I wanted to do for clients. "Building websites" is a very general description. I custom quoted every project that came my way, which was time-consuming and made sales harder. Getting specific about what I was offering and establishing pricing and packages helped streamline my entire client experience. It also helped with my confidence during sales calls, which meant I was booking projects at a much higher rate than before—even when I raised my prices.

After getting clear on what I was offering to clients, I built better systems to support it all. I started using a client management system to track leads and projects, and I created robust proposal and contract templates that I could easily adjust depending on the project. I mapped out every single step of my client process from lead to site launch, identifying where there was a disconnect or room for improvement. Establishing these systems cut down on the busy work that sucks so much time from our days, which made a world of difference when I added cyber-school teacher/facilitator to my list of responsibilities!

All of this was in place headed into 2020, so I had a steady, solid foundation for myself. Without it, I would have felt uncertain about continuing my business alongside everything else, and honestly, I may have given up entirely.

Setting Boundaries & Cutting Some Slack

Perhaps the biggest adjustment I had to make this year was with time management. I had gotten used to six-plus hour blocks within which I could prioritize and schedule my work. Then, whiplash style, I was back to the good ol' days of squeezing in email, design work, client site updates, and admin tasks in between Being A Mom. Except for this time, instead of changing diapers and fetching snacks, it was helping my son with cursive and making sure my 4th grader scanned in her math assignment.

I knew I had to get boundaries in place to protect my time and energy. I began pre-scheduling client phone calls so I could time-block work sessions without extra interruption. I removed my work email from my phone so I'd no longer get sucked into anything at 9pm. I even referred a few leads to other designers to make sure I didn't overcommit. Knowing when to say "No, thank you!" has become an incredibly valuable skill this year.

But the biggest boundary of all was, and is, the opposite of all that rigidity: being flexible and cutting myself some slack! I have always prioritized being responsive to client requests and aggressively attacking my To-Do lists. But this whole year has been an exercise in adjusting expectations and being comfortable with not always having everything done at the end of the day. I've had to lower my own standards (just a little!) and pay attention to my mental energy so I don't burn out. And it has been FINE. Clients are still getting what they need, and I'm incredibly proud of the websites I've been creating.

Something I think we've all been yearning for in the past year is hope. Perhaps my 2020 story shares a bit of hope in the idea of success even when life feels uncertain and out of our control. Being able to not just survive but thrive this year was definitely a surprise. I was accidentally prepared for running a business while homeschooling my kids, but I'm grateful for it! (I will also be grateful for the day my kids get on that school bus again!)

Bio

Photo by Shannon Confair

Jennifer Lyker, founder of Inksplash Designs, is a WordPress wizard and unapologetic Netflix binger who creates websites for busy and overwhelmed entrepreneurs. Through her 15+ years in business, she's helped hundreds of clients find their ideal clients, make more money, and reach their goals faster—all through their websites.

With her blend of web-geek expertise, eye for visual design, and done-with-you process, she helps entrepreneurs reclaim the time they spend fussing with and yelling at their websites.

Connect with Jennifer

www.inksplashdesigns.net

Instagram: www.instagram.com/inksplashdesigns

Facebook: www.facebook.com/InksplashDesigns

LinkedIn: www.linkedin.com/in/jenniferlyker/

FREE Website Launch Guide: An 8-Step System for Bringing Your Website to Life!

www.inksplashdesigns.net/website-launch-guide/

Website Content Planner: A simple do-it-yourself workbook for writing & organizing your website content

www.inksplashdesigns.net/website-content-planner/

Twenty Won

Strategy

Twenty Won

Leverage Your Soul-Level Magic

Cori Wamsley

I never intended to start a business, but it's always been a dream in the back of my mind. As a writer, I didn't know it was actually possible to do on my own because I never knew anyone else who did it.

On my youngest daughter's first birthday, in 2015, I got notice from my job that they were cutting all the senior staff. After ten years as a writer and editor for federal government agencies, I wasn't sure what to do. I certainly wasn't happy at work, and I longed for the freedom to write what I wanted, actually get a byline, and have more flexibility for my girls and my husband. That's when a friend suggested I do my own thing. So I did.

I started out thinking I would freelance part-time—since my girls were one and three at the time. My plan was to write all the pieces I was familiar with like web material, press releases, and blogs, but whenever I mentioned that I had authored five novels, other business owners were intrigued. "How do you write a book?" I came to find out that this was a mysterious science—alchemy—to others where it just came naturally to me. Turning words into gold was second nature, so I made it my primary business.

For the first four years, I grew slowly, taking on book-editing clients and developing my 1:1 and group coaching programs. Like many other people, I looked at 2020 with a hunger. This was going to be my year! I would finally start doing more speaking. I was to release my book on how to write a book for your business (*The SPARK Method*) in February. And I wanted to take the world by storm.

In March of 2020, I enrolled in a coaching program for speakers because I had goals to achieve. Two weeks later, the world shut down. My daughters were home from school . . . and not just hanging out. I had to teach a first grader and entertain a preschooler while my husband paced the house like a caged lion trying to figure out what was going to happen in his world, since he works in sports, and they were unsure if there would be a baseball season at all.

Work-life balance became a joke. I ate my feelings more than I should have. And my client base drastically changed. My group program had shown much promise, but suddenly, everyone who wanted to join was either "homeschooling," working a ton more because of their industry, or struggling to get by because their clients dried up. The strange thing is that the beginning of quarantine opened an opportunity for the perpetually busy people to start or finish their books, and that meant that I was inundated with editing requests by May, along with some fantastic, dedicated 1:1 clients who were determined to make the best of the strange opportunities in the 2020 landscape.

I rolled with it, and by summer, it seemed safe enough to bring in our amazing sitter, a high school girl down the street, to help out. As the daughter of a pharmacist, our sitter knew the dangers of the pandemic and was also taking all the safety precautions. Because of her, we were able to have some stability, let my daughters interact in person with another human they adore, and actually push forward with my business.

I boldly decided to start serious 1:1 work with a business coach I had been following in August and knew it was the right step to grow in a massive way. But 2020 decided to play another joke on us . . .

Editing hours are long and require a high level of focus, so I was thankful for the help from our sitter, especially when baseball surprised us by having a jam-packed season halfway through summer. Suddenly, our new normal was thrown into chaos again with my husband working five or six twelve-hour days a week from mid-July through the end of September. And our sitter had to quit working with us at the beginning of August because of a family vacation.

When the girls went back to school at the end of August, it was all I could do to keep my sanity as my husband and I juggled work and schoolwork. He was required to be in the studio at his TV station because he works in production, which you can't do from home. I, thankfully, work from home, but with a second grader and a kindergartener who aren't used to being on a computer all day, it meant that I had minute pockets of time to work, sometimes as little as ten minutes, before I needed to troubleshoot a school meeting glitch or help the little one with her letters. (Those "Js" can be sneaky, curvy beasts to write, you know.)

In the middle of all this, I fought fatigue most of the year, which I used to think was brought on by my allergies, especially ragweed in August and September. Typically, I spend those two months as a zombie anyway and just push through till it dies off and the weather gets cooler. In 2020, it seemed to be more stress-related though, along with stress headaches and an off-and-on issue with throat pain near my thyroid that shows up with even mild stress like a difficult workout or hearing my kids arguing. The stress of never knowing what was going on this year with school or work meant that the aching and tightness or swelling (I honestly don't know what it is) was so bad some days that I could barely speak.

By the time October rolled around, I wasn't sure I could keep going. I was so thankful that hockey didn't start right away, which allowed my family to get into a better pattern for our days with my husband working from home full-time on editing and having a lot of time off in October.

The additional clarity of coming out of the severe stress of September allowed me to focus more on what I wanted. I wanted to expand my team. I knew I couldn't keep pushing myself past the breaking point—let's be honest, health issues plus the anxiety of COVID and two small children remote learning is enough to get you to the breaking point without throwing being CEO on top of it.

My strategy was simple: 1) Bring on additional editors. 2) Adjust my programs to be exactly what people crave. 3) Adjust my pricing to aim at the right people for those programs. 4) Do every. single. thing. that my business coach told me to do. 5) Lean on my husband more. (He's part of the team, after all!)

I spotted a golden opportunity in the midst of the pandemic this October, and like Alexander Hamilton, I wasn't going to throw away my shot. (*Hamilton* came out on Disney+ in July of 2020, so it became our theme music for the rest of the year.)

As a woman, I sometimes find it hard to admit that I need help, but I knew that my goals wouldn't happen without it. Hiring my business coach over the summer allowed me to home in on the soul-level magic that I have for helping clients create books that share their transformational stories. In fact, you're reading one of them right now! And it helped me start to truly LOVE what I do as I gained confidence in my methods and leaned into my intuition when working with my clients.

I'm a good editor, and I always loved editing books. But in 2020, I realized that I needed help there too. I couldn't keep spending long days doing that type of work if I wanted to grow my business by building relationships. I needed to trust that amazing, talented people would work with me as editors for my clients, and guess what! I found some. I trusted my business coach to guide me on a process with that, and now, it's pretty smooth moving from coaching to editing to formatting to published.

I also had to put aside the mom guilt and let my husband help more. As the parent who works from home, I typically considered myself the "do everything that didn't get done" parent. But with my husband working from home, we got into a rhythm where we are both doing housework and homework without me feeling like, as the mom, I "should" be doing more. It takes a lot of discipline sometimes for me to stay in my office while my husband is cooking dinner or helping with math, but I had to understand that this is what it means to be a team, a couple that works toward a mutual goal of having a happy, loving, healthy family.

As a business owner, your magic lies in what drives you, your passion, your purpose. When you're pulled in too many directions or stray too far from what you love, that's when you'll find the most stress, the least trust, and the toughest climb to your goals. I'm hoping that 2020 presented challenges like we won't ever see again, but challenges will always pop up, no matter the size. My recommendation to you is to pull back from the heavy emotion surrounding a challenge and look at it objectively. That may take some time if it's new or particularly big.

Examine what the challenge means for you in the long run. Is it something you really need to address? Is it a nudge toward something simpler? Is it a sign that what you've been doing is no longer working? I firmly believe that things can be simple and streamlined, and I've always focused on working smarter not harder. You're in charge for a reason, so steer toward what you believe deep down will work as you navigate the challenge.

Acknowledge that you need help. When you want to do something you've never done before, seek out a coach or mentor. Contract out what isn't your zone of genius. Let your husband or kids take on some responsibilities. Sacrificing your health or sanity for your goals means you will backslide. Is it really worth it? Prioritize, divide, conquer. Besides, victory is much sweeter when it's shared.

Trust in your soul-level magic. When you think that the challenge is insurmountable, dig deep. Remember why you're doing what you're doing to begin with. Replay an exciting conversation with a client in your head. Look at your vision board or a picture of your favorite vacation spot. Remember that you wouldn't have desires if you couldn't make them happen. Open your heart, let your super powers flow, and climb that mountain.

If I've learned anything as a business owner, it's to believe in myself and the power that I have to truly make change in the world. The love I have for this planet and all its inhabitants great and small—especially a couple little sweeties with big dreams who I have the honor of raising—drives me to overcome my greatest fears to push forward with the dream I have for my business of working with men and women worldwide who want to make the world a better place. And we're doing it one book at a time.

Bio

Cori Wamsley is the CEO of Aurora Corialis Publishing, helping professionals tell their transformational story through brilliant books that help them cultivate relationships, make the change they want to see in the world, and reach their bigger business goals.

She is the creator of The SPARK Method of book writing, and her bestselling book *The SPARK Method: How to Write a Book for Your Business Fast* and her coaching programs help leaders

Photo by Dominique Murray

write and publish books that complement their brands and purposes. In the past five years, she has helped dozens of coaches, speakers, service providers, and nonprofit leaders develop the right books to boost their brands and build their careers.

Cori also wrote and self-published seven fiction books, including one with her daughter London when she was five. Cori is the former executive editor of *Inspiring Lives Magazine*.

Before starting her own business, Cori worked for ten years as a professional writer and editor for the Department of Energy and the Department of Justice. She holds a master's degree in

English literature and bachelor's degrees in biology and English literature.

Connect with Cori

www.coriwamsley.com

Facebook: Cori Wamsley

Facebook group:
www.facebook.com/groups/writethatbookbuildyourbusiness

LinkedIn: www.linkedin.com/in/cori-wamsley-667498112/

Instagram: www.instagram.com/coriwamsley/

Clubhouse: @coriwamsley

Book: http://bit.ly/SPARKbook

Free gift: Discover how to tell your story so your transformation impacts more people and helps you build your brand! www.coriwamsley.com/sell-with-story/

Resilience Revisited

Karen Captline

It was 2012. I was 43, married, and had a well-paying corporate job at Dick's Sporting Goods. Up until this point, working hard and working smart had worked just fine for me. I had worked my way through different positions, getting great reviews and promotions until I found myself in middle management. I tend to say that I had nine great years at Dick's—unfortunately, I was there for 12. Somewhere along the way, the company and I had lost our vibe, and I just worked harder to try to find it again. I had blown past "burnout" at least a year before, and was now in a moderate depression. I felt like a wife of an abusive husband—but surely we could find the love we once shared, right?

Wrong. The moment came. I was offered a job by a VP who had moved to another company. Still, I had to see if my "relationship" with Dick's was salvageable. I asked my director a series of questions, and when he answered the final one incorrectly, I gave him my two weeks' notice and, shaking, went to my cube to accept the offer from the other company.

My husband had wanted me to quit outright to fulfill my dream of being a freelance graphic designer, but like a codependent lover, I latched on to another corporate gig and jumped from the frying pan into the fire.

But that blaze burned out quickly. Things definitely weren't vibing there either. About two and a half months in, they fired the VP I had come to work with. About three months in, I gave them until December 20th (six weeks) to replace me. Then, on December 18th I learned that they were undoing everything the VP had done—including my department. I had to fire people days before Christmas. The universe was telling me in no uncertain terms that I should leave the corporate world.

So, you'd think I would have been joyful to start this new chapter. But if you've experienced depression, you know it doesn't work that way. My self-esteem was at an all-time low. Even if the choice to leave was mine, I felt that I had failed. They made me feel worthless, and it weighed heavily on me. After building my career for 20 years, leaving that part of it felt like a divorce. I felt guilt at having thrown away the things that others would kill for. I felt weak and stupid that I let the corporate world overwhelm me.

I would rage around the house as I did when I would come home from Dick's, continuing to take my stress out on my husband because I had nothing left to give. When anyone asked anything of me, I wanted to curl into a ball and hide—a side effect of the demands of the job and my own high standards.

Then a day came when I flew into road rage, and suddenly it hit me. Not a car, but a realization. "What do I have to be angry about? It's mid-morning, and I'm just going to the grocery store." I'm not *there* (at work) anymore. I pulled into the parking lot, shaking, as the most wonderful feeling of gratitude flowed through me. Things would change from that moment on.

I had been running from something, but now I would start moving with purpose toward my new life. I helped my educator husband organize the mess of a library he had taken over from a colleague. It gave my hands and mind something to focus on. I became a better domestic manager, purging and reorganizing the house as if exorcising demons. And I planned my future.

I took the experience and skills that I had gotten in the "divorce" and began stitching together a business with them. I organized the tools I had on hand and bought what I would need, including a new computer. Every purchase was triggering anxiety now that our household income had been cut by more than half. And I had no idea how I was going to find clients.

I focused on getting my marketing materials in line and pulling my portfolio together. I also set a target completion date for designing all the collateral for my brother's wedding— my gift to him and his new bride. Ever the marketer, I put my new logo and website address on the bottom of all the wedding favors, so I had to be ready by then.

And so, on August 23, 2013, BetterBe Creative Services was launched upon the world! Well, to about 125 wedding guests, but *still*. Photography was also part of my skill set, so I had taken some candids at their reception and loaded them into a gallery on my new website. People who wanted to see my photos of my brother's wedding would have to look at my new business too. *insert evil-plan laughter here*

By chance, the wedding coordinator for my brother's church was the same one that had coordinated my wedding 13 years before. She had started a cookie-baking business and was a member of a women's networking group. Shortly after our reconnection at my brother's wedding, she introduced me to Pittsburgh's women's networking world, where I would have to *gasp* talk about myself and my business! This wasn't easy when my self-confidence was so low, but it forced me out of my comfort zone and gave me knowledgeable and supportive women to learn from and lean on.

The universe now decided to show me, in no uncertain terms, that I was now on the right path. Before Dick's, for the first seven years of my career I worked for the riverboat attraction in Pittsburgh called the Gateway Clipper Fleet. My old boss still worked there and clicked my post through to the website. I got a message through my website saying, "I didn't know you were doing this! We were just going to look for a freelancer. We have projects for you!" Tears streamed down my face as I read it.

Confidence was ramping up. That first year I said YES to any opportunity that arose, challenging every corner of my comfort zone. And during this time, I was being told things by my old Dick's coworkers. . .

"They just hired *another* person to do just this portion of what you did."

"Your director just got demoted."

"I told three of your replacements that *combined* they didn't live up to what you used to do."

After a year and a half, five people had been hired to handle what I had handled alone. Meanwhile, my director and his VP had been fired. Oh, sweet karma. This was verification that, indeed, I had been treated unfairly and overworked to the breaking point.

But in March of 2014, the true purpose of the universe's swift kindness to my career was revealed. We lost my dad to complications from heart surgery. And now this new life allowed me to be there for my mom and my family. Building my business was a blessing to focus on as I moved forward. And more work came over the years. My clients and projects grew courtesy of my networking groups and particularly from an ex-boss who had moved on through several companies while I kept those clients in his wake. In the following six years, things were going very well via word of mouth and my network hustling. I kept my gratitude and added more self-care practices. Things were humming right along.

During 2019 I had put voice to trying to figure out how to "sit on my ass" and get new clients. Well, I had no idea that my powers of manifestation were so powerful. Sorry, world . . . Here comes 2020!

I was working with the Gateway Clipper to get their season started. Oops. Gathering on riverboats? Nope, shut it down. The huge convention I was working on the graphics for? Nope, thanks for playing. I began to realize that the eggs of my client base were heavily in the retail and entertainment basket.

My husband is an educator, so we were lucky to have a steady income, but a lot of my small businesses were going to be in trouble in the coming weeks. After a flurry of activity, incoming work got pretty slow pretty fast. So, in between the jobs I had, I focused on "those" projects. You know the ones, the ones you never seem to get done. Updating the portfolio/website. Cleaning up paperwork. Purging files. I pressured myself to get things done during the "two weeks to stop the spread." Then the length of quarantine turned into an open-ended proposition, and I had to come up with a new plan.

Creating a New Community

I started a Dick's Sporting Goods Alumni Facebook page. There had been a large layoff even before the pandemic, so I thought we could network and support each other! Ulterior motive: a lot of these people know what I have to offer. My posts would keep me at top of mind for any opportunities that arose.

Twenty Won

Creating a New Revenue Stream

Having used Shutterstock image services as my go-to graphic-design resource for so long, I decided to plunder the thousands of photos I had taken over the years, put them on there, and offer them for sale. Who knew a simple picture of corks would be popular in Canada, Mexico, Spain, and Australia? I know that now. Since then I have expanded my Shutterstock library of photos and graphics.

Creating New Services

For years I wanted to learn video editing. I started that process this year. I'm developing an idea to teach people how to use Canva. It seems counterintuitive, but if people are going to use it, they might as well learn it from me and learn some design basics to boot. I was thinking of calling it "What Would Karen Do?", but these days people would answer "ask for the manager." Maybe I'll still call it that if just for the laugh over my now-unfortunate name.

Focusing on What I Really Want

I discovered that I LOVE designing books and book covers. I told everyone who would listen. The more I talked about it, the more covers I would land. Books are pandemic-proof and help diversify my client roster. I look forward to expanding my opportunities in this sector.

Paying it Forward

For my clients hardest hit, I donated some time. For others, I pushed off sending invoices. I created manageable payment plans. I bartered. I prayed as I heard stories of unreasonable landlords and income streams drying up. I had a business to defend, and I wanted to help others defend theirs too.

Saying "YES"

Over the years, I focused on getting the best ROI, fighting my intense "fear of missing out," and more strategically expending my time and efforts. Maybe I played it safe in some cases. But in 2020, I got back to YES. That "yes" mentality is why you're reading this. Because I was enlisted to design the cover for this book, I was asked to be part of meetings with the authors Kelli had brought on board to this point. While listening to their stories, I realized I had something to say. I pitched Kelli my story, and she had one spot left. The universe was sending me signs again.

I am in the fortunate position of having an amazing supportive husband who also has an essential job. We have no kids, so we didn't have the added burden of homeschooling. Still, even for us, 2020 had been stressful and scary for many reasons. But when I felt the pull to despair, I focused on gratitude. I said YES to scary opportunities, like writing a chapter in a book.

Gratitude and "YES" are my two biggest gifts of 2020, and I hope you carry that forward into your future business and life endeavors.

Bio

Photo by Christopher Captline

Karen Captline started her career as a child, drawing on the backs of her dad's old accounting reports. After high school, she went on to attend the Art Institute of Pittsburgh, and her parents only asked that she not dye her hair any crazy colors. She went on to get her bachelor's degree at Point Park University where she met her future husband in a psychology class as she was trying to understand her parents' hair issues.

After an internship at Station Square Entertainment Complex in downtown Pittsburgh, she worked as the graphic designer at the Gateway Clipper Fleet riverboat company for the next seven years. Next, she worked at Dick's Sporting Goods' corporate office, where she advanced through various roles for the next 12 years.

Having gained enormous amounts of skill and experience, Karen decided to leave the corporate world and use all that knowledge to provide businesses of all sizes with design excellence and as much fun as possible!

Quick Facts

Personal style: Drama-free

Best use of creativity: Design and bad jokes

Vices: Musical theater and semi-pro shopping

Hogwarts house: Ravenclaw

www.betterbecreative.com

The Tools in my Tool Chest

Maartje Jorritsma van Krieken

"It is better to conquer yourself than win a thousand battles. Then the victory is yours. It cannot be taken from you, not by angels or by demons, heaven or hell."

- Buddha

The awfulness of 2020 for me started the dreaded moment we got off the plane in Pittsburgh on January 6th. Here I was, after two glorious weeks in my happy place with some of my favorite people and endless champagne powder to ski in, back in the place I did not want to be. Back in the place where I had no professional identity, had struggled to build a social life, was homesick for the first time in my life, and felt utterly lost, alone, and very raw from the sudden loss of my Aunt Agnes—whose love helped me keep my demons at bay. I was in a very dark place, and this was even before COVID-19 turned all our lives upside down.

But here I am in January of 2021, barred from travelling to recharge over the holidays in my happy place with some of my

58

favorite people, still hurting from losing Aunt Agnes, still homesick for almost any place, and yet . . . feeling like I won. I won against my demons; I managed to climb up and off the slippery slide down and put myself back on a path where I see light, opportunities, and progress to realizing my dreams. I won because I conquered myself.

Lost

2020 was my perfect storm, which had built up gradually over the second half of 2019. I had resigned from an almost 20-year, dynamic, successful corporate career in the summer of 2018. I was, and am, very content with that decision. I was also very happy and grateful for the free year I spent after—a "nap year" when I chipped away at my own pace through a still-growing bucket list. By the summer of 2019 I was ready to get moving with "professional Maartje 2.0" and had somewhat of an outline and a too-long list of opportunities to try out. As an impatient woman, the moment I am ready, I need to be moving at a breakneck speed. Instead, due to an amazing opportunity for my husband, I suddenly ended up in completely unknown Pittsburgh, being what I always vowed to never be—just "the wife" and "mother". I feel like a monster admitting this, as I truly believe I have the best husband ever, a true-life partner; I want to be at peace for him, being here for his amazing professional opportunity. I equally believe my kids are the best thing in my life; they make me understand what a bursting heart feels like, all the time.

However, I have always liked school, my studies, and my work—a huge chunk of my identity has always been my professional me, which was not visible to anyone I met in

Twenty Won

Pittsburgh. Since I left home for the university 25 years ago, my work (and studies) has always been intertwined with my lifestyle, my social life, and later, even my parenting. For the first time in over 10 major moves in those 25 years, this interconnected web was broken—I came here without an anchor of my own. I struggled without my friends, struggled giving shape to my professional plans in a city I knew nothing about, where I had no network and no purpose to my days. I struggled with how much we were to invest locally, considering our relatively temporary stay here. I felt invisible and non-existent.

With everything I tried, it felt like there were mainly failures, indecisions, or desperate choices. I became more disillusioned, my childhood demons started to rear their ugly heads, and my confidence was crumbling fast. And then, by early December, I lost my Aunt Agnes, the one who could help me rein in these demons.

By February 2020 I was hanging on by a thread, escaping with weekend trips to visit my friends elsewhere. Walking around with my "soul under my arm" as they say in the Netherlands, I tried to shore up my smile and maintain an upbeat attitude when I did find the energy to try and meet people. And then it was Friday the 13th, March: Lockdowns were announced. Our tickets to Europe were cancelled along with all the weekends away that should and would have energized me. Our visa renewal process was halted, jeopardizing our immigration status for months on end, causing loss of my work permit and stopping the just-planted seeds of a new social life from taking root.

Rock Bottom

By April 2020 all our plans were well and truly cancelled. Any notion the pandemic would be a short-term thing was duly obliterated. It had become clear that a decision on if and when our visa would be renewed was months and months away, and the kids would not go back to school the rest of the school year. We had not seen any other people in six weeks. I wanted to give in; I was empty, tired, done. The tears were coming, my chest tightening up. As I was ready to surrender out loud, I looked at the kids and my husband watching a movie and thought, *I am back on that slope!*

Almost 20 years ago my husband and I went skiing here in the US. He has skied his whole life and is very, very skilled. I however was still a beginner though his father and friends had taught me some in the weeks we spent with them in their family ski-place in the Alps. As it was just the two of us this time, we sometimes would split up, allowing my husband to do a few diamond runs, whilst I would stick to some of the easier slopes. Somehow, I ended up off-piste—between the trees—in a place where nobody else appeared to pass.

The slope was too steep and icy, nobody knew where I was, I was starting to panic, and the tears started coming. And somehow in that moment, my brain sternly said to me: "STOP! Giving in to the panic is not going to do anything for you; you are the only one who can get yourself out of this." And just like that, calm certainty took over. I defogged my goggles and started to think about the tools in my tool chest. What did I know? What were the tools I had to save myself? My father-in-law's voice entered my head as I focused on a safer point ahead and started a very slow, controlled slide down the ice. By the time I linked up again with my husband 30 minutes later, I was elated and high on adrenaline; I had conquered myself!

There in my living room in Pittsburgh, feeling scared, depleted, and lost, I was back on that slope, and the calm certainty came over me. I had to pull this krewe (New Orleans speak for "crew" or "club") through the summer ahead with their sanity intact; if I would not step up to the plate, nobody else would.

Plotting a Course

The calm certainty stayed with me for a few days, and with the tools in my tool chest, I cobbled a plan together. What did I know about the things that would soothe my family, distract and energize them? I am the queen of planning family adventures and living life to the max. I just needed to work my magic within the new constraints. We needed to see other people, so I started to look for COVID summer buddies— friends to form longer COVID bubbles with so we could have some normal human interaction which we all so craved. What could we build on to create some purpose and routine, some things to look forward to? What would we do if we would get kicked out of the country? What did our plan B look like? And with every piece that started to fall in place, more opportunities became apparent.

With increased confidence that everyone else was going to be okay, my eyes also started to open toward the tools I already had in my tool chest to sort myself out. I started to see that, despite being miserable, I had made some great choices already for me to build on. I had turned my volunteering at United Way into a paid role, working directly with the COVID response when the pandemic hit, which was enormously satisfying and provided commitments to others pulling me through the apathy. I was doing a coaching certification course with some great peers and had started to use the practice sessions more effectively to tackle the issues at hand while relishing the (virtual) social interaction that grew from getting to know each other better every week. I realized the blessing from working for a nonprofit would be that I could continue working with them when my work permit would expire, back as a volunteer. And by seeing other people again, I saw myself through their eyes, and my confidence, at last, stopped crumbling. I started to be in control of my demons again.

Winning

By the time the kids started school again in September, it felt like we had not only conquered the pandemic summer, but truly made some superb lemonade out of the COVID lemons. We still had no news on our visas, missed all our friends and family abroad, and knew that our time with the friends in our summer bubble had come to an end with everyone going back to their own homes and commitments in other states. Yet, we also knew we had cracked the nut on how to do this as a family. And we didn't just hang in there, we thrived despite what the pandemic, an election year, and an overdue racial justice reckoning were doing to life as we knew it. We were winning as a family while I felt I was winning as a mom and partner—doing right by the ones I love. I started to believe that if I could do this for others, maybe, I could also do this for me.

Twenty Won

And back to my tool chest I went. I imagined the icy ski slope between the trees to be me looking down and out toward this place of professional contentment. If nobody else was going to come and rescue me, what tools did I already have to rescue myself? What would I need to make it past the slippery slope? I needed deadlines; I needed a feedback loop; I needed interaction with people who could be critical on my plans without jeopardizing emotional safety; I needed help asking for help; and I needed to feel like I was in motion. Beyond the icy slope is the space where I am effective managing my demons and where the good days outnumber the bad days.

So, out of the tool chest came my network—someone to team up with for weekly accountability sessions, accomplishing the tasks I set out to get to Professional Maartje 2.0. I slowly started reconnecting with people for sparring and peer challenge sessions, daring to put my work and ideas in front of others again, getting help erasing the unhelpful self-censorship, and starting to trust in my own superpowers again. I started to accept the help offered and build on the opportunities my current work and new coaching certification offered me. I had a treasure trove of saved articles, podcasts, and TED talks in my tool chest that I finally tapped into to find some fresh inspiration and energizers. And despite still feeling lonely, uncertain, and too invisible; despite failing frequently in my trials; despite post-COVID life not appearing on the horizon yet and missing my friends more and more each day; I made it in only a few weeks down the icy slope.

Won

I won in 2020. I won because Professional Maartje 2.0 is here. I am professionally satisfied with the path I am on and the mix on my plate as a Change Maker in an industry that makes a difference, as a career dynamics coach and mentor for a select set of clients, and as an emerging writer and speaker with some gigs on the books and something new in the works in the Diversity & Inclusion space. I am back to making "five-year plans" and in motion daily. But my most precious win has been the conquest over me. I would not want to do it again on my own, but now I know I can. I conquered me, by myself.

Bio

Maartje is a change maker, combining project and change management experience with decision quality, synthesizing, and facilitation skills; a drive that moves mountains; and brilliance at a Human level.

This mother of three worked 20 years in the male-dominated upstream oil and gas industry internationally, opting recently for a career pivot to independent executive consultant, certified coach, and a corporate diversity and inclusion offering.

Photo by Malathi Machani

Twenty years ago, Maartje left the Netherlands (where she grew up) for good, moving around the globe and working on every continent. In the United States she lost her heart to New Orleans where her love for a social life on steroids, living life for today; glitter; costume and décor making; good food, music, and art; and functional chaos all perfectly fell into place. She is learning to love Pittsburgh and actively plotting "where next" in this life.

Maartje is a qualified skipper and capable scuba diver, skier, and paddle boarder, happiest when she is sharing life with friends and/or can feel the sea breeze in her face.

Connect with Maartje

www.dmaartje.com
LinkedIn: www.linkedin.com/in/maartje

Twenty Won

Inspiration

Twenty Won

From Imposter to Inspiration

Kelli A. Komondor

I was always expected to go to college, graduate with honors, and get a "good job." I was supposed to get a four-year degree and "make something of myself." That path may have been the obvious route to take, but the road I ended up on would take me on a more scenic route to discovering who I was really meant to be—and what I was meant to do.

I spent all 12 years of elementary and high school in the gifted program and truly was a creative kid. I got straight A's until middle school when it became more important to be popular. My grades slipped, and I didn't graduate with as many accolades that had been expected. I did enroll in the community college, but I didn't know what I wanted to be when I grew up. During one college semester, I was taking business courses, an English course that I loved, and pharmaceutical math . . . at the same time. My parents were frustrated with my lack of direction, I'm sure.

Tired of not knowing what to do, I took a semester off (you know where this ends) and picked up more hours at my hospital food service job. Within a year I was married and had my first child— a son we named Cameron. It wasn't the path anyone expected for me; but it was the one that felt right. I was twenty-two and in love with the two most amazing guys in the world—my husband and son. Three years later our little family was complete when Kayla entered the world on a cold Sunday afternoon. I was where I was supposed to be. I had two healthy, beautiful children, a husband who supported us, and many loved ones in my life. I didn't need college and I didn't work for a few years—my family kept me busy enough and I was happy.

Looking back, I was truly thankful for every job I had over the years—from a fire hall "bingo girl" (which is how I met my husband . . . another story for another book) to positions in the retail, food service, and medical sectors. I moved into the corporate world in 2004 and spent 16 years working in publishing, IT, and banking with "prestigious" job titles. I worked hard and was even promoted multiple times while in the publishing industry. I made great friends and built a trusted network of professional connections. But inside, I was struggling. Although I was mostly happy in those jobs, I was still on the hunt for something better, be it more money, a better title, or a more progressive company. I had been turned down for so many interviews because I didn't have a degree. I once told a recruiter that my decade-plus of experience, my work ethic, and my connections outweighed a piece of paper I would've earned in 1994. And I asked her to relay that to the hiring manager. I rarely had a hard time getting the initial call—it always came down to that degree. It worked against my confidence. It made me feel that I would never have better opportunities, and it even affected me in the jobs I already had. Sometimes I was afraid to speak up with an idea or join in conversations. What if I said something stupid? What if they asked me questions that I couldn't answer?

I wasn't exactly sure what to think about how I was feeling until a dear friend and mentor told me that I was suffering from "imposter syndrome." I had feelings of inadequacy that persisted despite having success. I suffered from self-doubt and felt "less than" because of not having a degree—and often working with and being surrounded by many people who did made me constantly question my skills and ability.

Those thoughts of doubt flooded my mind and not only affected my professional life, but also my personal life and my health. Late in 2019 I told my friends and family that 2020 was going to be "The Year of Kelli." (Little did I know what 2020 was going to look like!) I had been diagnosed with Type II Diabetes in December of 2019, and I knew that I had to make A LOT of changes to get my health back on track and to get my professional life in order. I started 2020 in the position I had been in for nearly three years, and one that I loved—until I didn't. Being unhappy with your job is probably one of the worst things ever. The crazy thing is that I was successful the prior year, I was learning a whole new industry, I was surrounded by colleagues who believed in me, and I was hired by a kind and caring manager who knew I could do the job — without a degree. It just wasn't what I wanted to do. I took a new position that seemed like a perfect fit but one I discovered just wasn't right for me. I made the best of it for about six weeks . . .

Then COVID.

I was laid off. I came home, applied for unemployment, and then thought, What now? I spent the next few weeks starting indoor seedlings for our garden, cleaning out some closets, reading a few books, spending lots of time cooking with my husband, writing a few pieces (one that was published), and walking nearly every day. This was exactly what I needed— freedom to get outside and exercise and to stop the terrible eating habits I had adopted while working 10-hour days. No more of the countless lunch appointments, eating fast food on the fly between meetings, and inhaling appetizers and wine at evening networking events.

On those daily walks, I found myself thinking more and more about what my next move needed to be . . . But that imposter syndrome kept nagging at me. Could I do it? Was I good enough? I always dreamt of being a writer. I grew up creating notebooks full of never-completed novels and teen angst poetry, long gone in some landfill. I knew it was now or never . . . so, when I was called back to work in May—I declined.

Again, "What now?" I knew I didn't want to look for another job. I was staying home and staying safe, and I had no interest in taking a position where I'd be working with the public or forced to report to an office. My health had become too important to me. Plus—what was out there? Who was hiring? I spent the next four weeks researching; talking to friends who were business owners; coming up with a logo, a name, and a tagline; building a website; and writing somewhat of a business plan. I pulled out books written by female entrepreneurs and read over notes from marketing seminars I had attended over the years. I lost sleep, I fretted over every detail, I wrote and rewrote emails and text messages to friends, made endless lists of what I needed and wanted to do . . .

And then I just did it.

In June 2020 I launched K2 Creative, LLC. I knew from the many years I spent working with small business owners that they had so much knowledge about their industry. They had incredible stories to tell about their companies; they simply didn't know how to tell them. Whether it was lack of skills, lack of time—or both, they didn't share enough. My mission became helping them with clear, consistent messaging, which involves social media management, improving their website content, blogging, e-Newsletters, email campaigns, creating press releases, and providing PR services. I do what they considered "busy work" or things they do to check off their list because someone told them they should. I provide a digital presence, and they continue to run and build their businesses. At the time I'm writing this, I have over a half-dozen monthly clients, and I've had a handful of one-off writing projects. We turned our son's old bedroom into my office. My commute is mere footsteps, and my mental and physical health have improved immensely.

2020 did turn out to be The Year of Kelli. I've learned what and how much to eat, and I am walking about 20 miles a week.

(Those changes have contributed to a 30+ pound weight loss!) I was able to stop insulin injections back in April 2020—just four months after my diabetes diagnosis, and my oral meds were cut in half shortly after. While my body feels great, there are still days my mind tells me I don't deserve any of this happiness or success. But I'm working on that. I remind myself daily that I have people who are depending on me, people who are expecting me to put my best foot forward and turn their thoughts into words and ultimately help them share their knowledge and grow their businesses. There is no room for me to doubt my ability; I just don't have time for it.

I don't like telling people the pandemic was the catalyst to starting my business. As I type this, on Inauguration Day 2021, people are still dying from COVID. People are losing their jobs and their homes. Businesses that have been here for generations are shutting their doors. It's never-ending sadness and gloom most days. It's hard to stomach.

I try to keep telling myself: Sometimes bad things must happen before good things can.

So, what's the lesson? What's the takeaway from a girl who grew up in a little Pennsylvania river town called Glassport, never finished college, raised a family, started a small business during a global pandemic, and then created an anthology with twenty other women who made the best of one of the worst years in history?

Simply said, "If I can do it, you can too."

I know it's cliché. I know you always hear it when you are trying to lose weight, get a promotion, complete a task that seems impossible. There's always "that person" telling you how they overcame a difficult situation and came out on top.

Today, I'm that person. Today, I'm your inspiration.

Listen to your gut—mentally and physically. Recognize that you have one life, and no one can make it your best life but you. You deserve to feel good. You deserve happiness. There are so many resources out there—use them. You have twenty-one women right here in this book who have taken a leap and done something scary but amazing. We are a diverse group of women, from the color of our skin to our birthplaces, ages, upbringing, backgrounds, education, experiences, and lifestyles. We are as different as they come, yet we all have something in common: the strength and determination to be successful and happy.

I know you do too.

5 Inspiring Ideas When Starting Your Business

Carry a notebook. Only write things pertaining to your business in it. Keep it on your nightstand and jot down anything and everything that comes to mind. The first entry should be what you want to do, who your clients will be, and why there is a need for what you're offering. And in this notebook, you must make lists! Not only will they keep you organized, but they'll also keep you mindful—and you'll feel so amazing each time you cross something off!

Follow the leaders. Find publications and white papers written by successful women in business. If you find someone in the industry you're entering, that's a bonus! Look for inspiration!

Read and research. Use government sites to make sure your business name isn't taken. If you don't know where to start in creating a website, or if you don't know much about social media, Google will be your best friend. There are endless resources—use them!

Let go. The best investment I've made so far is hiring a bookkeeper—and you'll meet her in this book! Recognize immediately what you should let go of (make it a list!). You will learn quickly that you can't, and you shouldn't, be everything in your business. If you don't have the ability to do something, don't waste time and energy—hire out.

Connect. I can't tell you enough how important it is for you to build a great professional network and connect with people. Truly connect. I'm not talking about collecting as many business cards as you can at a networking mixer. Get to know people. Every client I have has been a result of who I know. I can attest to the saying, "It's not always WHAT you know; it's WHO you know."

Bio

Photo by Salene Rae Mazur Kraemer

Kelli Komondor is the president and CEO of K2 Creative—a content, marketing, and branding firm helping small businesses and nonprofits "Make Their Message Matter."

Her diverse professional background includes writing and storytelling, PR and communications, team leadership and management, marketing and new business development, and event planning and execution.

In 2020, the year of necessary changes for small businesses, nonprofits, and corporations, Kelli found the courage to follow her dreams–to start her business and become a published author. She is the creator and project manager of *Twenty Won.*

Kelli is a lover of love, writing, and food—and a hater of hate, chaos, and stemless wine glasses. She lives in a little borough called Port Vue with her husband, Rob, and their Yorkie Poo, Mia. Her most successful venture to date is raising their two compassionate and intelligent children—Cameron and Kayla. In her free time, you'll find her cooking and entertaining, reading food labels, drinking wine, walking, cheering on the Steelers, and "picking" at garage sales and antique shops.

Her immediate goals are to continue to write, grow her business, and help others.

Connect with Kelli

Website: www.K2CreativeLLC.com

Website: www.KelliKomondor.com

Email: Kelli@K2CreativeLLC.com

Clubhouse: @KelliK2C

LinkedIn: www.linkedin.com/in/kellikomondor/

Instagram: www.instagram.com/k2creativellc/

Facebook: www.facebook.com/K2CreativeLLC

Did You Count the Hard Stuff in that Gratitude List?

Jessi Wagner

"But I have a master's degree. Shouldn't I use it?"

That's what I kept telling myself when I was ready to make the transition to leave my career. After all, I had already totally changed directions from the teaching career I thought I would have my entire life to being a mental health and drug/alcohol therapist. I thought that was exactly what I wanted. Yet, as my health-and-wellness business (that started out as a side gig) grew to bring in a full-time income, I realized this wasn't the life I wanted. I LOVED my work as a therapist, but I wanted to own my time. I wanted to plan work around my life instead of life around my work. I considered many options of work in the field, but as I reflected a little more, I realized I was desperately searching for a job description that made me feel like I didn't waste my time in grad school and that would look good to other people.

Twenty Won

I thought about what I REALLY wanted to do. I wanted to empower women to own their lives, know their worth, and live authentically and fully. I wanted to teach women what I know about being your healthiest self—physically, mentally, emotionally, spiritually. I wanted to spend time volunteering and advocating for what's important to me.

It was then that I realized my health-and-wellness business was exactly what I needed in that moment, but I also knew there would be more. I am so passionate about mental health and social justice, and I knew that I would be somewhere in that arena one day, just not confined in an office. At that moment, I wanted to spend more time with my daughter, appreciate and enjoy what I'd built, and trust that, with that leap of faith, the rest would come to me.

Leaving a job I loved was really really really hard, but I also felt this overwhelming sense of peace that I was doing the right thing. After about two years of disappointment trying to get pregnant with our second child, we conceived just two weeks after I left my career. I don't believe that anything is a coincidence.

It was an amazing nine months. We had just bought my grandparents' home. My Nana passed a few years before, and I loved that I was raising my family in her home. I felt her with me more than I ever had. The house had the most perfect home office I could ever dream of. I had an amazing morning routine that filled my cup every day before Hannah got up. I LOVED my days with her. I would go to the gym every day, and she played in the daycare, waiting for me. I loved that she got to play with other kids but spent most of her days with me.

We took music class, swim lessons, and did so many fun things. We even went to Disney World. Obsessed with owning my time, you could not have paid me enough to go back to working for someone else. I felt like I had the absolute best of both worlds. I was able to be with Hannah as much as I wanted, but I also got to step away, own my identity outside of being a mother, build my own empire, and still significantly contribute to my family financially. I felt like I had a perfect work life balance and was truly living my best life.

I had a super healthy pregnancy. We were so grateful and ready to welcome Logan into our lives. Admittedly, I was also really anxious. I had wanted another baby SO badly, but I LOVED my life the way it was right now. I was afraid of how bringing a baby into the world would shake things up. Though Logan was due on the 4th of July, I was so set on him coming sooner. I didn't know that that would be the first of MANY expectations I had that didn't go as planned. Logan finally arrived an entire week later on July 11, 2019. In business terms, that's almost halfway through the month, and I felt like I wasted the first 11 days being anxious about when the baby would come. I needed to have this baby and get back to work. After all, things were so different this time around.

This "fourth trimester" wasn't the same as the one I had with Hannah. With her, the maternity leave was an amazing break. I loved the paycheck I was getting from my side business because I didn't get paid leave as a teacher. I loved being able to spend more time on my business since I didn't have my full-time job to worry about. I was able to be present and bond with Hannah. I had lots of support, and I LOVED being a new mom.

Twenty Won

This time around, my side business had become a huge source of income for my family. I felt so much pressure (from myself) to maintain my income and be an example to other moms of what was possible. This time, my time and attention had to be split between two children. This time, the baby never slept and never let me put him down—and I was drowning. My morning routine that I was so attached to was shot. I felt like my house was falling apart and that running my business was impossible. Meanwhile, my mental health was taking a huge toll. I was in a tornado of doubt, fear, insecurity, guilt, shame, and hopelessness. I felt like I would never be enough for everyone.

It was a really weird sensation. As a clinician, I felt like I was outside of myself, diagnosing myself with postpartum depression. As a wife, mom, leader, daughter, and friend, I thought I could just power through and work harder, and eventually things would get better.

I was wrong. I was so wrong. Things just kept getting harder. But I realized that I had tools. I knew what to do to at least make myself a little bit better: I had to constantly change my thoughts. I had to constantly tell myself that I was enough. I had to constantly validate to myself that THIS IS SO HARD. I had to constantly tell myself that it was okay to not enjoy every second. I leaned HARD on my friends that understood what I was going through. Most importantly, I wasn't afraid to say I was struggling.

As I opened up about my struggles and allowed myself to be vulnerable, I realized I was giving permission to other moms to admit their struggles and find solidarity. I realized that the problem was not necessarily the struggles but the fact that no one was talking about it.

We put all these unrealistic expectations on ourselves because we think that somehow everyone else is doing it better than us, that everyone else is able to do it all, but we just can't. Even logically knowing that that is simply not true, it felt impossible to overcome the guilt and shame in my head, especially when most of what I was seeing on social media was the highlight reels of other moms who were "doing it all."

So, I decided to start talking. I wanted to start getting involved with maternal mental health advocacy. Starting to realize that I was going through this for a reason, I became grateful for it and inspired to use my story to help other mothers. Then, while in the shower, my only quiet time to myself on any given day, it hit me: I needed to create a deck of affirmation cards for mothers. ALL mothers, struggling with postpartum or not, need to reaffirm to themselves on a daily basis how incredible they are. Mom guilt and mom shame are SO real. If we aren't constantly changing that story, it will slowly creep in again. These cards could be a simple way for mothers to do that when it feels impossible to do on their own.

A few months later, in May of 2020, my first 100 decks of Mama Mantras were printed, and I immediately began selling them on Etsy.

My favorite part of Mama Mantras is that they are helping mamas everywhere take one small, easy step to practice self-care that EVERY mama has time for. We are always told to practice self-care as if we can just snap our fingers and be in a bubble bath with candles, music, and a good book. When you're in the thick of it, self-care can seem next to impossible. What I've found is that self-care happens in the smallest moments. Self-care happens in your head when you're changing your thoughts. Self-care happens when you choose to implement healthy boundaries. It happens when you release judgment of yourself and other mamas. It happens when you make healthy choices. It happens when you allow yourself to feel your emotions. Self-care happens when you learn to be grateful for ALL the hard stuff too—and that is one of the biggest lessons that I've learned.

Currently reaching mamas in over 70 cities, more than 20 US states, and four different countries, Mama Mantras has already grown and changed in so many ways since the beginning, while I have learned so much in the process. I've added a second edition, Mama Mantras for the Mompreneur, and a third edition, Mini Mantras for kids. Having become more connected to resources and individuals in the maternal mental health arena, I also serve as a volunteer mentor for new mamas through NurturePA. And none of this would have been possible without a postpartum experience that almost took my life.

Life, business, motherhood . . . It won't always be rainbows and butterflies, but each moment is valuable. When you have learned to find gratitude in the hard stuff and trust that something good is coming from it, you will begin to change the way you look at things, and your whole world will change.

Everyone had to find ways to pivot in 2020—learning how to work virtually, getting creative and innovative, etc. However, my struggles in 2020 didn't come from my businesses being impacted as much as it came from putting everyone and everything else before myself. I had to pivot by finding new ways to cope with stress and proactively take care of myself. I had to pivot by deciding to control what I could—and surrender the rest. I had to pivot by choosing to take one small step toward a better feeling and forgive myself each and every single time I fell back into old thought and behavior patterns. I had to pivot by choosing to love myself.

This whole experience has taught me more than I could have ever imagined. I learned that my story is important, and the world needs me—my whole, imperfect, authentic self—to share it. I learned to TRULY be grateful for ALL the "hard" because without it, I wouldn't be where I am today. I can genuinely say now that postpartum depression was one of the best things that ever happened to me. Building my health-and-wellness business in the beginning was HARD. When I started in 2015, I was working full-time, I was in grad school full-time, and I had another part-time job (and there were so many more transitions along the way). Still, I KNEW in my heart that it would be worth it. I knew that I was meant for so much more than the mundane life that I was living, and SO ARE YOU.

Because I was brave enough to take that leap of faith, a passion I never knew would exist was eventually born. And today I am able to serve others in a way bigger way than I ever imagined, which has always been my goal since I was a little child—I just didn't know exactly what it would look like. I don't know exactly what it will look like in 5, 10, 20 years from now either.

Twenty Won

What I do know is that I'm going to keep showing up because I am worth it, and YOU are worth it. There will be messiness and heartbreak and success and joy, but it will be so worth it. And I can always choose to find hope and gratitude in every single moment.

Bio

Photo by Mia DeMeo Photography

Jessi Wagner is a wife and mother of two who started her career life as a teacher before transitioning to a mental health and drug/alcohol therapist. Jessi has always been passionate about helping others, but as her career evolved, she realized there was no job description that allowed her to truly serve in a way that felt authentic and aligned with her values. When the opportunity to run a health-and-wellness business alongside her career was presented to her, she thought it could be the vehicle to feel fulfilled while also owning her time and her life.

However, two years into her business, she walked away from her career, knowing that there would be more in store for her in a way she didn't yet know. Although she didn't expect it would come from a traumatizing postpartum journey, Jessi was able to turn her struggles into a gift for other mothers in the form of Mama Mantras. Now, Jessi is grateful that the experience led her to be the advocate for maternal mental health that she is today and use Mama Mantras to empower other mothers to live authentically and love themselves fully.

Twenty Won

Connect with Jessi

Please connect with me on social! I would love to meet you and hear your story!

Instagram:

@jessi_wagner_
@mama_mantras_

Warriors do What it Takes to Make it Possible

Brandi J. Lipford

So, in 2021, for most of us, it got off to a rocky start. Perhaps it was downright ugly to a lot of us. However, we, as women, are resilient. I'd like to call us "warriors." A "warrior" is defined as a person who is strong and refuses to give up easily. For those of us that you may have already read about, their narratives have been just that. Our stories just have been told in different ways. One thing stands out in all of us: We stand in the struggle; we find that WE are natural-born hustlers. We are all warriors!

My name is Brandi. Most just call me B, or Jeneen, which is my middle name. Let's see. . . I'm 46, a mom and a grandmother, a college graduate, yada . . . yada . . . yada. Let's get to the good parts, right? I love to travel, I'm a huge Steelers fan, and I enjoy being in my kitchen. Some say my baking skills are pretty decent too—though it may cause a cavity or two! I'd like to be introduced in this chapter as one of those warriors. I grew up in Pittsburgh and was raised by my grandmother and my mom. I'd say I had a halfway-decent upbringing. I saw what my gram and mom had to endure raising me. My mom was a police dispatcher, and my grandmother was a certified nurse assistant. They both were employed as (what we know these days as) "essential" workers. Life didn't appear to be bad growing up even though we were poor. My mom and grandmother did their very best to make the most out of a grim situation. That's probably who I learned my strength and resilience from.

Currently, I work in the airline industry for a major airline carrier as a customer service agent. You can call me the average aviation geek. I get to work around different types of aircrafts, and I absolutely love what I do! The perks of the job aren't too bad either. I get to travel around the world for free (on standby of course, but who cares?). Even though my job with my airline is secure for now, I work in an industry that is very uncertain. My carrier said that they will be ready to return about 400 pilots back to work by the summer of 2021—which is awesome news! There may be profit and an increase in travel as more people receive their COVID-19 vaccinations.

So, back to the title of this chapter . . . warriors do what it takes to make it possible. Ask yourself, in the nature of this pandemic, are you doing what it takes to make it possible in your world? For me, even though I have a secure W-9 position, I still would like to have other streams of income. I have always had that entrepreneurial spirit within me, and sometimes I feel that my creativity does not support or fit my corporate environment.

Back in October of 2020, in between my hectic work schedule and baking, I did some research on how to start up an LLC. I used my stimulus monies to help pay for my filing fees. With the pandemic slowing down some filing procedures with state documents, I was able to pick and choose a name for my LLC, appoint myself as a registered agent of the LLC, file the Certificate of Organization, prep the operating agreement, and apply for my employer identification number. Within a month, BJL Enterprises, LLC was born! This is a limited liability corporation under the principal of real estate, public relations, and event management. I will focus on areas of real estate closings as a notary and also dabble in real estate investments. I also plan on using this platform to book speaking engagements and manage virtual events, webinars, town halls, and planning services.

I had been using all of these wonderful and talented gifts for others for years, so why not for myself? As far as other things I see in the future with this LLC, I got plans . . . lol! I have already networked with a few individuals who are helping me connect with different local programs of interest that can carry me to the next level. That said, I have access to these programs and will utilize them to my advantage. I took a low-cost real estate development investment course, invested in becoming a notary for my LLC, and created a website to display what BJL Enterprises, LLC offers. Trust and believe, with my business, the possibilities are endless.

Even though you may be a savvy entrepreneur, you will still need help to be successful along your path. I've also enlisted a few accountability partners to help me stay the course of meeting my goals along the way. Sign up with your local government for community resources for small business. Your local universities have programs that have free and low-cost training and resources for small businesses as well. The purpose of you being a successful entrepreneur is that you simply have qualities that others do not. Entrepreneurs don't just think about doing that idea, we actually execute it. We take action until our idea becomes reality. It's the fire; it's our drive; it's the challenge.

Let me share with you my warrior story and what I had to do to make it possible:

I thought I had life all figured out in the late 90s, settling into a career that I was enjoying as a paralegal. You know the basics: drafting legal documents and pleadings, including deposition notices, subpoenas, motions, contracts, briefs, and complaints. However, behind the scenes I was tackling a puzzling health challenge. Growing up, I had always dealt with headaches of some type—some minor and others not so minor. I was diagnosed with migraines. I was pretty good with being my own health advocate. I went to all of my scheduled appointments, and nothing major stuck out about these headaches. One day in December of 2003, I had this headache that no medicine could cure, with other serious symptoms including hearing loss, vision loss, frequent nose bleeds, and fainting spells. When I reported these symptoms to my primary care physician, she ignored me. She told me it was stress due to my job and attributed to being a single parent.

Really?

I requested to see another doctor in the practice and scheduled another appointment. When I went to see my new doctor, I explained to her my symptoms and my disdain with the previous doctor not taking my symptoms seriously. She listened. After our initial appointment, she ordered me to have an MRI (with and without contrast along with a chest X-ray) and requested to have those notes and scans sent over to her immediately. The next morning, she called me personally and asked me to come in before the office opened so she could share what she had learned. She explained that I had complete obstruction of my brain fluid, which was probably the reason why I was feeling so much pain; they were pressurized headaches. She also said that the same scan showed what she thought was a small tumor. Expressing that she was not as knowledgeable about neurological matters, my new doctor referred me to the neurosurgery department where, she said, I would probably need brain surgery in the near future.

My heart sank.

At first, I was like, wait . . . what? She didn't just say what I thought she said—but she did. Those words would forever change my life. I took a deep breath and cried for a bit. Then I collected myself and made those important phone calls to my close family and my employer.

After I met with my PCP, I was then scheduled to see a neurosurgeon who explained to me that I had what's called Chiari Malformation—a birth defect in which brain tissue extends into the spinal canal. When this section of your skull containing a part of your brain is too small or is deformed, it puts pressure on and crowds your brain. The lower part of the cerebellum is displaced into your upper spinal canal. If Chiari is not diagnosed at birth, it usually presents itself during the third or fourth decade of life. For me, I was just 29 when I was diagnosed.

The headaches that I was experiencing? My brain had no room! I had pressure-like headaches that would worsen when I coughed or sneezed, neck and shoulder pain, and irritating ringing in both ears. Sometimes, I had difficulty swallowing, fainting spells, trouble concentrating, insomnia, and clumsiness, to list a few other symptoms. The brainstem is responsible for most body functions, so Chiari causes all kinds of strange symptoms. Back then, it was explained to me that I would always be under the care of a neurosurgeon and a neurologist. My first surgery, a decompression surgery, which took place in 2004, was a very painful experience and took me about nine months to recover from. My second surgery, which was an Endoscopic Ventriculostomy in 2005, was done as minimally invasive as possible and was not as painful as the first.

By this time, I had already resigned from my full-time job as a paralegal. I did need some type of income to help keep the household running. I started watching the neighborhood kids after school. What I didn't know was that you can't just watch kids without having a license. I researched how to have a licensed daycare home, and I completed the training along with the house being inspected. My first stay-at-home gig, and it was official: Brandi's Family Day Care was born! This was something that I could handle while still being at home and maintaining the bills. I enjoyed the kids that I watched, and they loved their environment. I also made my own schedule which made it easy for me to continue keeping up with my doctor appointments.

As I began to pick up the pieces to rebuild my life, I realized that I had survived. I am still surviving. I survive Chiari daily. I've had three more surgeries since 2005, the last surgery taking place in 2012. I'm not healed just because I had surgery. Those surgeries were merely maintenance. If you look at me, I look like a normal middle-aged woman. I have what's called an invisible handicap. You know, I "don't look sick," but if you could feel my facial pain and headaches, you'd realize that I am sick.

Here is where we insert "warrior." Every year that goes by without a surgery is a small victory for me. 2021 marks year number nine post-surgery!!! I share that little piece about me to convey that, even in the midst of this pandemic affecting us in ways that we could never imagine, think about this:

Life is short. Don't sweat the small stuff.

Whatever you've been meaning to do, please DO IT! That business you wanted to start, that dress you wanted to buy, or that dessert you've been wanting to order. DO NOT WAIT!

Sometimes you have to stop yourself from worrying, wondering, and doubting.

AND . . . things will work out. Maybe not the way YOU planned, but just how it was meant to be.

Making the best of it is just exactly what the doctor ordered. What I'm about to share with you will be the key to your success. Make sure that you get yourself a journal or a small notebook so you are able to keep track of your goals/wish list. The reason I say this—and this might make the little hairs on the back of your neck stand up—is that I made several entries that were faith-based. On December 1, 2020, I wrote that this next level that GOD is about to take me to is unimaginable. It's going to require that he has my undivided attention because, with the COMING ATTRACTIONS, there can be no DISTRACTIONS.

Shortly before the 2020 Christmas holiday, I was asked to be a contributor to this wonderful idea of a book that would showcase 20 other talented "warriors" like myself who dared to start up their business and/or nonprofits during the pandemic of 2020.

If you're lucky enough to be reading this chapter, well . . . you already know what happened next!

So, newly minted and armored warrior, let's be friends! Reach out to me on social media.

Bio

Photo by Brandon R. Lipford

Brandi's creative talents have been exercised across many different areas for over 20 years. Utilizing her strategic planning abilities, she's acted as director of special events—responsible for major events with the most noted names in the entertainment industry, including multiplatinum artists Jill Scott and The Whispers, Soul Train Award winner and smooth jazz artist Boney James, 16-time Grammy Award winner Kirk Franklin along with comedians Mike Epps, Katt Williams, and Kevin Hart, to name a few.

It doesn't stop there for Brandi. Her work with numerous nonprofit organizations like The Lupus Foundation and Community Empowerment Association as well as her experience in catering, sales, marketing, and event management has allowed her to develop her talents that ultimately led to the start (in 2020) of BJL Enterprises, LLC— a brand synonymous with prestige, strength, and excellence.

However, she's not all work and no play! Brandi is a die-hard Steelers fan as well as an avid aviation geek, so much so that she scored a part-time position for a major airline carrier as a gate agent. A home-and-garden fashionista, she's also a woman who can bake up a mean chocolate cake!

Twenty Won

Never forgetting the most important aspects of life—love and family, Brandi uses her talents and personal struggles to instill a sense of value in every individual she crosses paths with. She's not afraid to share with you that she is a five-time brain surgery survivor. The last thing you will do is feel sorry for this soul, but you will see the positive energy that she exudes in her journey—and be inspired by her walk!

Connect with Brandi

Email: lipbrand@bjlenterprisesll.com
Instagram: @ms._b_li

Faith

Twenty Won

It's All Through Faith & Gratitude

Lori Ball

Ahhhh . . . the year 2020 . . . the excitement of turning the calendar page. The anticipation of new beginnings, fresh starts, resolutions, and everything else that comes with "new." The year 2020 had such an ease about it; it rolled off the tongue. So easy, so positive sounding, like 2020 eyesight— perfect, right? Well, that's what I wanted the new year to be— perfect.

My name is Lori Ball, and I am founder and partner of Faith & Gratitude, a nonprofit organization with a mission of empowering and educating cancer patients. Working with patients and caregivers alike to promote empowerment is a cornerstone to our organization. Knowing we can all take an active role in our healing is not only empowering but needed. The mind, body, and spirit work together in divine synergy.

Twenty Won

As 2020 began, our nonprofit was embarking on its third year of operation, and we were anxious to get going, energized with the prospect of creating new and innovative in-person cancer wellness events along with other pop-up gatherings for those newly diagnosed was top of mind. Our early-year planning meeting came and went, and we were optimistic with what we had on the calendar.

Shortly after "perfecting" our calendar like so many other nonprofits do, we were unexpectedly faced with a major challenge. That challenge was COVID-19—a pandemic of all things! Wait! What?? A pandemic in 2020?? Talk about unsettling. This certainly wasn't what we had envisioned for the year, but who could have foreseen this situation? We wondered just how it would impact our organization— from patient events to our loyal donors.

We were quickly reminded that, even in the midst of a pandemic, cancer diagnoses do not come to a screeching halt— and neither would we. Determined and focused, our mission became even more resolute. We immediately made the decision to shift from in-person cancer-wellness events to virtual events. But exactly how would this be done?

We promptly pivoted and began researching virtual events and how to best accommodate our patient wellness model. Thinking these types of gatherings would be something we'd consider "down the road," in the blink of an eye they became THE only method we would have to reach our audience. Our commitment to cancer patients and loyal supporters grew stronger and stronger. We decided to provide online forums featuring national integrative cancer experts, and immediately our virtual Cancer Wellness Speaker Series bloomed. We were blessed to have met many speakers in the prior two years and felt comfortable enough to reach out to them. All three said, "Yes," and we were on our way to developing a new and improved message delivery system! Cancer patients from across the globe were able to participate—far more reaching than just hosting geographic centric venues in and around Southwestern Pennsylvania. Looking back, this may have been a blessing in disguise. Not unlike other businesses or nonprofits, the model was transformed, and maybe that's a good thing. Thankfully, the Speaker Series went extremely well and will now become part of our annual events calendar. Talk about making lemonade out of lemons!

By now, you may be wondering how Faith & Gratitude came to be? Well, establishing a nonprofit was certainly not on my radar, but I have learned that life has a way of peppering many little "dots" along the way until such time when those dots are able to be connected. This is something my sister-in-law shared with me: Be patient until you can connect the dots.

Like many other people, my life drastically changed in ways I could not have possibly envisioned when diagnosed with ovarian cancer in December of 2015. Through faith in God and faith in myself while finding something every single day for which to be grateful, I knew this was not to be my last chapter but, in actuality, just the beginning of a new chapter. What I could accomplish for other newly diagnosed cancer patients as they began their own personal cancer journey would be much larger than even I would have imagined, and that propelled me.

Twenty Won

The inspiration to establish the nonprofit came about after talking with many other cancer patients who, like me, felt as though there should be something more they could be doing for themselves while awaiting the next test, surgery, or chemotherapy/radiation treatment. Really looking for a holistic approach to healing became so important to me. It just made sense that healing the entire body, mind, and spirit when faced with cancer was paramount. Since this was top of mind, I quickly learned that many others felt the very same way. Oncologists have their plans to treat the disease, but looking to complementary modalities in order to keep our immune system as strong as possible during toxic treatments is vitally important. That is what Faith & Gratitude is all about—encouraging patients to look outside traditional standards of care, to research, and to become empowered.

In retrospect, my adult life had been riddled with signs, or "Godwinks" if you will. I always felt like my path wasn't quite the right path and a major adjustment was needed. I couldn't put my finger on it until a series of serendipitous events caused me to take a deep breath, sit back, and wonder. You see, for a very long time, I felt the strong desire to help people. I had no idea what it meant until my 50th year . . .

People close to me know I believe coincidences are truly affirmations, so when my 50th birthday came and several telling events happened, I unsurprisingly disregarded them and continued pushing forward. Looking back, it's quite clear these signs were put in my path to cause me to pause. But I didn't listen to my inner voice.

And then, in August of 2015, I was offered what appeared to be the perfect job opportunity that would take me to retirement. Our only child was just beginning his senior year of high school and would be heading off to college the following August. Perfect timing, right?

In retrospect, I now see that what I thought was the perfect scenario was really the perfect storm. I accepted the job, but the stress level associated with my new role began to take its toll on my body, manifesting in the forms of lower back pain, lower pelvic pressure, frequent bathroom visits, and the overwhelming feeling that something was off. My sense was that my dear father in heaven was talking with God saying that He must get my attention. In fact, I could strongly hear my dad saying, "Once again, she thinks she's on the right path, but she isn't. We don't want to kill her, but we must get her attention." And wow, I got the message, loud and clear.

Like it was yesterday, I recall that cold day in December when I found myself along with my husband in an oncologist's office—facing an ovarian cancer diagnosis. To say that moment was surreal doesn't even capture it. My husband used "gut punch" to explain his feelings. And I get it. You see, when cancer strikes, it affects not only that person but his or her family and friends. I am so thankful to all who continue to support me today. I am forever grateful!

Ovarian cancer is often called "the silent killer," but through the grace of God, I picked up on the symptoms quite early and acted promptly. I am confident that, in my case, this early detection was extremely important to the recovery I gratefully am enjoying today.

Twenty Won

More than ever, I am confident the work we do at Faith & Gratitude is my life's mission. I am incredibly thankful to have this opportunity to help others make the transition from cancer patients to cancer survivors who thrive in life. Awakening the body's innate ability to heal using the mind, body, and spirit connection is nothing short of empowering, and I am honored to walk alongside anyone who is newly diagnosed.

One of my favorite quotes is by Bernice Johnson Reagon: "Life's challenges are not supposed to paralyze you; they're supposed to help you discover who you are." Challenges in life are to be expected but often come at the most inopportune times. Or do they?

Since my diagnosis in 2015 and more recently the pandemic of 2020, it's become clear to me that we must be able to pivot on a moment's notice. Remember to think clearly, to remain focused, and to take the time to just sit back, breathe, and reassess. This can make all the difference.

I would love to connect with you. If you feel the same, please reach out to me. We have many resources available to those facing a cancer diagnosis, including our inspirational Cancer Resource Guide. Our Guide is free of charge to those newly diagnosed and is full of organizational and educational information that is sure to empower! It is everything I wish I had when I was traversing my own cancer journey.

In faith & gratitude

~ Lori

Bio

Photo by CJ's Photography

Lori Ball is a cancer survivor and the founder and partner of Faith & Gratitude, a nonprofit organization providing empowerment and education to cancer patients and caregivers. She always felt an intrinsic desire to help people, but the path to that end always seemed a bit blurry. That is, until the autumn of 2015. Not a believer in coincidences, when she faced her own cancer diagnosis, she just knew "this was it"—the turning point in her life.

Understanding the connection between the mind, body, and spirit—especially when faced with a health crisis—Lori has made it her mission to bridge the gap between the traditional standard of cancer treatment and a more holistic approach. Lori has worked in business for over 20 years and is now focused on growing her nonprofit where her vision sets the course for the organization.

Lori and her husband Dave live in Southwestern Pennsylvania, near Pittsburgh. Together they have one child, a son named Joshua.

Twenty Won

Connect with Lori

www.faithandgratitude.org
Email: Lori@faithandgratitude.org
LinkedIn: www.linkedin.com/in/lori-ball
Facebook: www.facebook.com/faithandgratitudeinc

A Difficult Time Leading to Being a Blessing to Others

Megan Fleming

All my life I have had a desire to help and serve other people. I grew up wanting to be a teacher (the ideal "helping" profession) and went to college to do so. I started teaching elementary school straight out of college and truly enjoyed supporting, teaching, and growing with my students. Even with the many challenges, it was a fantastic feeling when we emerged on the other side of the challenge having found a solution. And working with students and their families—I often got to help be a part of helping parents connect with their students academically or figure out better ways for them to be successful in school.

But about nine years in, having had my first child, I began to really sense the undergirding feeling that I was missing out on his childhood, development, and learning. I mean, I was a teacher, but I felt like I taught and helped others all day and then my energy tank was empty when I got home to be with him.

So, my husband and I began re-evaluating what we were doing as well as all our financial decisions. Through a lot of prayer and searching for different opportunities, we eventually made the decision for me to quit my job after the 2018-2019 school year and stay home with our kids (we now had our second child). But what would we do about the income gap we were creating? Moving to a house with a smaller mortgage and my husband getting a better-paying job helped but didn't accomplish it all.

Rewind a few months to a conversation with a friend of mine about how she started a bookkeeping business three years prior. She now had six kids, her husband was working part time while attending seminary, and it was helping them tremendously financially. At first, I saw the price tag of the training course (I knew nothing about bookkeeping before now, so I would DEFINITELY need some training) and politely said, "No, thank you."

I pursued some different opportunities to make some income, but nothing else panned out. So, when I asked around for ideas and help, my friend came back to me and encouraged me to consider it again, saying she thought I would be really good at it and how it could really be a blessing to my family. (Boy, was she right!)

This time I actually listened, asked more questions, talked a lot about it with my husband, prayed about it, and decided I would move forward in pursuing bookkeeping. I started the course in May 2019 and worked diligently on it through the summer, finishing in August of 2019. I felt very overwhelmed about starting my own business, so I reached out to my friend and shared my concerns.

(Starting a business is NOT for the faint of heart . . .)

She listened patiently and then offered to take me on in a subcontracting capacity so I could apply my skills and learn more under her (someone who had been in this field three years now). I began working for her, and that was a great start for me. I learned and grew immensely under her! I took on another subcontracting project later that year and then realized I wanted to have my own business. Working for others was very instrumental in guiding me to where I needed to be—owning and running my own bookkeeping business.

In January 2020 I officially launched my business and signed my very first client. She was (and still is) a fantastic client! I was able to help and assist her in getting her previous year cleaned up, which is often a daunting task. I supported and helped her transition from trying to do it all herself to having the weight taken off her shoulders so she could do more of what she loved within her business.

At this point, my first client was a substantial one and was fulfilling the financial need that my family had despite me quitting my job. I didn't really market my business or look for more clients. I was grateful for what I had and content in that place.

But then COVID . . .

Twenty Won

No one could have convinced me of what was coming before it did. But it certainly provided some opportunity to be a blessing to others!

In May of 2020, a local nonprofit reached out and asked for help with the Paycheck Protection Program loan. This led to a discussion about monthly bookkeeping support, and they signed on as a monthly client that same month—IN THE MIDST OF COVID. Another moment to help and support others.

Nonprofits took some hits in this pandemic when many had their livelihoods threatened/taken away, because what do people do when their income is cut? They stop giving. We worked hard together to cut expenses back and really monitor this nonprofit's budget, and consequently, they have been able to keep their business up and running (though a bit modified) through it all. This was yet another chance to come alongside a local business and support others.

During the summer of 2020, my husband and I started dreaming. What if we grew the business? This business was already creating a way for us to accomplish our goal of me being home with my kids and homeschooling. What if we were able to help other moms be able to be home with their kids? Could this business grow to where we could hire other moms and help them provide the income their families needed?

The dream was just beginning then and continued to grow over the next few months.

I began marketing online as much as I could. No one could really go much of anywhere during the pandemic. And even if I could have gotten out more, trying to professionally discuss business with two kids in tow isn't ideal.

As I began my marketing efforts, my first new client I found was Kelli Komondor of K2 Creative, LLC (the dreamer of and project manager of this book). She had recently started her business and I felt truly honored to be able to support her in getting everything in order with bookkeeping. Yet again, I encountered a chance to be a blessing to a new business owner.

Another new business owner was next who, like Kelli, wanted things to be in order as she began ramping up her business. She was leaving the college level teaching world to run a business. Despite the COVID restrictions, many people were starting businesses. And business owners needed good bookkeeping to keep their businesses open and thriving.

One more client signed on in 2020 as well. Surprisingly, she was opening a brick-and-mortar location during the pandemic! But because of that, she did not have time to be sitting in front of a computer and managing the bookkeeping. So, yet another chance to aid a business owner who was growing and thriving within her business.

Amidst all of the difficulties that arose in 2020 with COVID-job loss, stay-at-home orders, families and friends not being able to spend time together, my business still flourished. And I am truly grateful for that. But more importantly, I was able to be a blessing to my clients. And that is one of the best feelings—something that has been ingrained in me since I was small.

For the future of my business, I hope to continue supporting and helping many more in 2021 and beyond. More new clients are already arriving, and new partnerships beginning. I truly hope that they feel supported and in a better place with their business as a result of working with me.

My biggest hope for the future, though, is that through my growth, I can hire subcontractors—other moms—to work for me. I know what a tremendous help this business and its financial benefits have been for my family. I would be absolutely thrilled and honored to allow other moms to be able to make that decision to be home with their kiddos as well.

Who knew, at the beginning of 2020 when I launched my business, what would be coming in just a few months? I sure didn't, but taking over bookkeeping duties for business owners let me help others who are beginning their own businesses and those who are scaling and growing their businesses.

As I reflect on the steps it took for me to get to this place in business, I am reminded of all the ways others were constant and steadfast in their willingness to help me. Some allowed me to work for them while assisting me in growing my skills. Others answered questions and mentored me as I walked through the growing pains of getting my business going.

My greatest hope and prayer is that I can serve and support others as much or more than I have been served by others. The year of 2020 was a challenging one for sure. But I am emerging from it seeing all of the wonderful events that occurred for me. I look forward to 2021 (and beyond) in hopes that I can stay focused on helping others, both business owners and possible contractors that work for me.

To be the blessing to them that others have been for me.

Bio

Megan Fleming, owner of Cardinal Financial Solutions— Bookkeeping Made Easy, lives in Southern Indiana with her husband, Adam, and two children, Jonathan and Maddy Grace. She is actively involved in her church and their Classical Conversations homeschool co-op. Having taught elementary-aged children in public school, she left teaching in 2019 to come home so that she could raise and homeschool her children.

Photo by Beth Sumners

She began her bookkeeping business in 2020 to continue helping others—this time helping business owners. Megan enjoys keeping the books in order while helping business owners know their numbers, stay organized, improve their processes, and help their businesses grow and thrive. She hopes to be able to hire other stay-at-home moms to help them achieve the same freedom of being home with their children that she did.

While homeschooling, raising children, and running her business keeps her quite busy, Megan also enjoys reading, shopping, being active with her family, and finding new places to travel to and explore.

Connect with Megan

www.cardinalfinancialsolutions.com/
www.facebook.com/cfsbookkeeping/
www.linkedin.com/in/megan-fleming-3005b918b/

You Can Do HARD Things!

Racquelle Pakutz

Thank you for supporting us and reading our stories! My driving force to share my journey is **YOU**!

We are all unique humans and have a beautiful story to tell. I hope that this inspires you to keep pushing through whatever life throws at you and know that it is in the journey that you find what you are longing for. I am so honored and grateful to share these lessons acquired during my warrior journey.

Learning to embrace all that happens in life and go with the flow while being true to who I am has been SUCH an amazing journey! In looking back at 2020 and the challenges and obstacles in the world, in my home, and in my internal self, I am now even more in amazement of what one can truly do!

I believe you CAN do anything, but it all begins with the thoughts that are happening inside your head. This is my first lesson to share: **pay attention in the morning**—when you first wake up each day you begin to think and create the experiences in your world. I believe the BEST advice I can share to light the pathway through entrepreneurship is to cultivate a daily routine of self-care and self-awareness so these early morning thoughts can work for you, not against you.

The path of an entrepreneur is one that is not for the faint of heart: you must be your own badass hero every single day. Sometimes, this alone is challenging enough, but then if you have employees, you have a BIGGER responsibility to show up as your best self each day. Now you must focus on the way you WANT to be seen for the business while also embodying what your employees NEED to see so they feel like they have a strong leader and vision to follow—even if that is not how you, the business owner/leader, are feeling inside.

2020 challenged me in more ways than I ever thought possible—from facing social isolation; to growing a new business and the fear of failure that comes with it; to becoming a mentor and a leader; to cultivating mindfulness while bringing it to everyday life. Being isolated with your family and trying to lead and be positive during a global pandemic is freaking HARD. But anything worth doing is going to be HARD. I am here to tell you that YOU CAN DO HARD THINGS! All beginnings start out hard, but with practice, consistency, and determination, they get easier over time.

The first challenge in 2020 was navigating a work-life balance when it was all one and the same. March 1, 2020, mere DAYS before the shutdown, was the day I officially hired my husband, Jon, and our daughter, Mesa, full time to work with me at Zen Freight Solutions. This was a HUGE step and a leap of faith, but it all worked out in the end.

I had to battle myself in my mind every single day in the early part of the COVID outbreak to get up and keep going. Some days were better than others, but I found that, through cultivating gratitude each day and staying connected with others, I felt okay. Hiking through the woods became my daily routine. Every morning, I would leave the house listening to morning affirmations, inspirational speakers, and new self-development books. I found hiking in nature to be a simple way to escape from the pressures of life. While on my daily hiking adventures, I found peace in the solitude of nature. I found myself, and I found God.

You have to get away from the world, get really quiet, and just listen. Listen to your thoughts, listen to your breath, and listen to the beautiful world around you. Something magical happens when you spend time under the trees amongst the untouched natural beauty of life surrounding you.

Starting off my day with a hike in the woods with positive thoughts was a huge help, but it did not solve the feelings of isolation. I knew I had a good start to my day, but I needed something more. Not only were we isolated from our friends and family, but we were isolated professionally as well. All networking events were cancelled, any client meetups were postponed, and all summer fun was seemingly extinguished.

As a startup company, networking events were the best way I knew of to get our name out there, and suddenly there was nothing. So, I joined a few online group meetups. I feel extremely fortunate that I was introduced to a local nonprofit, eforever.org, that helps small businesses work on their business with their peers. We met monthly via Zoom where we connected with one another and kept accountability for reaching our goals. I cannot even explain how helpful and refreshing it was to connect with and relate to others while navigating the tough times. There is power in community and knowing that you are not alone. I also joined another online meetup of logistics professionals that met every Friday at 1pm via Zoom and streamed live on LinkedIn for others to join the fun. This helped me feel less isolated, more connected, and like part of a community while I stayed home, which helped rejuvenate me and guide me each day.

We took another leap of faith so we could safely visit clients across the USA during COVID: we purchased a camper. This involved many trials to make sure it would work for the whole family, starting small with three test runs in Pennsylvania campgrounds before packing up three adults, two dogs, and a cat and traveling farther.

On top of the online social community and traveling office of sorts, I also found a network of local women who I joined (and continue to join as often as I can) to partake in yoga, sound healing, and nature therapy. Joining a community of like-minded women was my saving grace from deep depression and personal isolation.

Thinking about the tools that helped me get through the frustration and isolation of the pandemic reminded me of how I became an entrepreneur in the first place. In 2018, long before the pandemic hit, I was living life on autopilot, stuck in a corporate job without the confidence to step outside my comfort zone. Someone mentioned that I could learn new skills and that all I needed to do was look for opportunities to learn them! Somehow, after 10 years of being out of college, I had forgotten what it felt like to learn new information. I have to say that audiobooks and YouTube changed my life! Once I started listening to inspirational messages and positive affirmations, it was like a waterfall of knowledge, and I've never looked back!

When starting my business in July 2019 I took several long months to work on myself and my mindset. The work I did and the habits I built were extremely important in 2020 as I continued to surround myself with the greatest minds I could find and continued to stay inspired despite the adversity of owning a small business during a pandemic. To date, I have read over 48 books on Audible and consumed over 2,000 hours of inspirational messages through podcasts, speakers, and training online!

I also took advantage of the nothingness of 2020 to advance myself professionally. I am a board member and student for the George Washington University Customer Experience certificate program. Yet another amazing opportunity to connect with like-minded professionals, in all markets, all over the United States, this program gave me something to focus on during the long nights isolated at home by giving additional structure, community, and support.

"Have patience and engage in consistent action!"

– Les Brown

(This is a Google calendar reminder that pops up on my phone every single day.)

Learning to be in the present moment and not caught up in thoughts of the past or the future is THE MOST important lesson thus far in my life. I have realized that we only ever have the present moment, and when it is gone, it is gone forever. The biggest lesson of 2020 is that time does not stop even if the world as you know it does. Change is difficult but necessary to stay in the present. If you cling to the thoughts or beliefs of the past, you risk living in a state of suffering. If you worry about the future and play endless possibilities, your mind gets trapped in what I call "the hole." This is a place of fear, overwhelm, and worry, and it too will make you suffer. The only answer is to be in the present. The only answer is to live your life exactly how you want it to be right here and right now. The only answer is gentle kindness, love, gratitude, and hope.

It has taken a lot of daily practice, devotion, and compassion with myself to learn that the fear-based perspective does not serve me. When I am in a responsive state, I am not my best self. So, what do I do when I start my day stressed out and negative? I TAKE CHARGE of my emotions and energy and become mindful of my thoughts. I then focus on the positives in my routine, like peace and safety. By following a set schedule, treating my body like a temple, and only fueling health and not disease, I can be my absolute best self. In this self, I am equipped for the day and in the right mindset to handle anything that comes my way!

It has taken a lot of trial and error, long days, recording and reviewing things that didn't work, and practicing the things that did work. I am by NO MEANS saying this is the only way. This is my personal belief and toolbox. I hope that this can be a starting light for your path, because I know that as you learn to walk in the dark, you will eventually create your own light.

As entrepreneurs, it is written on our hearts to do something AMAZING. You have an OUTSTANDING talent, and I believe you will succeed. You create the world you live in, one thought at a time. Please use this as a guide to staying in the present moment and creating the best future self that you are.

I want to leave you with a simple tool I use daily: **WARM.**

W – Wake up with Gratitude

First thing when your eyes open, give thanks. Take five minutes to be grateful for your life and all that you are. Gratitude is the pathway to your soul.

A – Affirmations and Visualizations

Next, (before you look at your phone and contemplate your life) go through your affirmation list. If you don't have one, listen to some on YouTube, and eventually you'll create your own! While you are affirming yourself and your goals, visualize yourself where you want to be, where you are going. This practice can shift your perspective instantaneously.

R- Raise your Heartrate through Body Movement!

This one is self-explanatory; I like to hike, but anything to get your body moving is great! Maybe you like to sing and dance in the shower or go to the gym. That is great too! The goal is to move and enjoy it!

M- Mind your Body

This is the most important step and should occur in the morning and throughout the day: Be sure you are fueling your body with positive thoughts and clean foods as much as possible.

Bio

Photo by Alisha Graham

Racquelle Pakutz is the president of Zen Freight Solutions Inc., founder of Healthy Happy Hiker, wife, mother, and healer. She began her business journey a few short weeks after graduating with a B.A. in business management, which she earned over the course of two and a half years. This, of course, was made possible by the fact that she LOVES to learn. This ambition to fill her mind flourished through the opportunities that were in front of her in the logistics field.

After gaining a decade-plus of experience in logistics, learning the ups and downs and rights and wrongs, she chose to leave the corporate world to focus on her health, family, and quality of life. This would mark the start of a new way of life, including healthy living, mindfulness, self-love, and entrepreneurship. She constantly strives to grow and evolve herself and her portfolio every single day.

From books to magnificent future business ventures, stay tuned to her family's journey to learn more about what is possible—and maybe even a little more about yourself!

Connect with Racquelle

LinkedIn: Racquelle Pakutz
www.linkedin.com/in/racquelle-pakutz-366b666a
Facebook: @healthyhappyhiker
www.zenfreightsolutions.com

I Chose Happy!

Maria Theresa Bernardo Brady

So, who is this jovial person writing a chapter in a book about successful businesswomen? Well, I am a fun-loving mom and GiGi (aka Glamorous Grandma) who enjoys gathering with friends, meeting new people, and wearing trendy fashions! I am energized when surrounded by people, whether it's social time or work-related. I embrace positivity, find the blessing in every situation, and as a cancer survivor, know the importance of choosing happy.

First, I want to share my heritage, which influenced who I am today. From the 1930s through the 1950s, my paternal grandfather, Anthony, and my paternal grandmother, Theresa, who is my namesake, each owned restaurants. Their entrepreneurial spirit was passed down to my father, Tony. Ironically (this book being about surviving 2020), my maternal grandmother, Mary, miraculously survived the Spanish flu in 1918. While she was eight months pregnant, her husband died from the flu, leaving her to raise a newborn and three young children on her own. Her positivity and resiliency lived on in my mom, Dorothy.

My dad earned a GED, and my mother only completed 8th grade, but to meet them, you would think they graduated from Harvard. They understood hard work, but more importantly, they understood people. They built an iconic restaurant in McKeesport—a small steel town along the river near Pittsburgh, Pa. Although the population and steel industry declined, their delicious food and authentic love for their patrons sustained them. A national burger chain closed, but my parents' restaurant thrived! My loving, gifted, faithful parents were rewarded with the success of enjoying their life's work. Happily living by example, they instilled in me the spirit of entrepreneurism and the resiliency to achieve my dreams.

Fast forward to 1996: I am a college graduate, married, mom to our first daughter, Rachael, and gainfully employed as a bank marketing officer. I cried every day going to the office, longing for precious time with my beautiful toddler. My core value of "family first" was not aligning with my reality. A flexible work schedule was not an option. The technology tools of today, such as the Internet and email, were just being launched, so working from home was unheard of. The conservative approach of playing it safe, collecting the paycheck, and embracing the 9-to-5 grind—not for this gal! With two initial clients, a computer, a phone, dial-up Internet (LOL), a fax, and a lot of courage, I left the bank marketing world and founded my own marketing agency. I chose me!

Choosing me meant that I was solely responsible for my paycheck. There was no paid time off, no paid health benefits, and no retirement contributions. Financially, I would initially lose so much on paper, but what was my true desire? Priceless time! I wanted to be a mom enjoying a flexible work schedule while engaging in work that was my passion. I truly believed my business would grow.

We welcomed our second daughter, Kailey, in 1998. Juggling two kids and a growing business was challenging, but I had the support of my husband, Ed, and my mom who loved babysitting her granddaughters! Late-night writing sessions, while my little girls slept, afforded me awesome playtime during the day. Within three years, my client base expanded to a national level. Within five years, I acquired our first international client. How, you may ask? Well, before I answer, let me share my cancer experience that insightfully parallels my business success.

Intuitively, as a strong woman and entrepreneur, I knew to pursue medical care. Something was not right. In October 2013, my doctor phoned to say my bone-marrow results revealed I had a rare blood cancer called Waldenstrom's Macroglobulinemia, a form of non-Hodgkin's Lymphoma. He said, "It is incurable, but treatable. Typical life expectancy is 5-7 years. See you next week for chemotherapy." Wait! What? The shock was indescribable. But with conviction, I declared that I would live well beyond that life expectancy!

A second doctor advised that we watch and wait. I chose to BE WELL not DWELL. I chose to define my life—to not allow cancer to define me. That positivity and a healthy lifestyle contributed to a delay in my treatment for six years. From March through August 2019, weekly infusions of chemotherapy and immunotherapy became part of my schedule. I approached managing my cancer like a work project. What's the ultimate goal? Remission. What are the tactics? Stay healthy, choose happy by focusing on my blessings, remain strong, and be faithful. On Thursdays, I blocked off time for my all-day infusions, allowing for a reduced work schedule on Friday followed by the weekend for recovery.

During treatment, I met all my clients' deadlines and traveled for work engagements. For six months, I participated in an exclusive Women in Business Cohort at Chatham University to identify business growth areas. Also, I was featured on the cover of an industry magazine showcasing my creative talents.

On August 14th, I triumphantly rang "the bell" after ending six months of therapies. Tears of achievement fell while my heart pounded with joy! However, in November, three months post chemo, remission had not occurred. Intravenous immunotherapy continued into 2020 during a pandemic, which was very mentally and physically challenging. I stayed centered on the present. In August 2020, as I felt the treatment's ill effects, I decided holistic healing was my new path. I knew who my mentor would be.

Serendipitously, in 2018, through a dear friend who survived ovarian cancer, I met Lori Ball, founder of Faith & Gratitude. I financially contributed to her impressive nonprofit. As a cancer survivor, Lori's mission is to empower and educate cancer patients. Little did I know that chance encounter would play such a pivotal role in my life. Lori educated me on holistic practices such as pulsed electromagnetic field therapy (PEMF), meditation, and healing frequency music. I greatly reduced stress by eliminating the news and other negative sources. I cannot control the disarray of the world, but I can focus on being mindful.

My perseverance and positivity are paying off. I am now in remission! When I chose me, I knew I could beat cancer, just as I believed in me when launching my agency in 1996. In 2021, Marakae Marketing celebrates 25 years in business. So, how was I able to grow my agency and provide for my family for a quarter of a century? My inherent success factors in business and fighting cancer are parallel—starting with people, rooted in the love of my family, and reinforced through faith, perseverance, resiliency, intuitiveness, and positivity.

People

I extend my sincere gratitude to my amazing team that brings my ideas to life. My agency thrives because of their dedication. I value my clients who trust me to contribute to the growth of their companies. My business model is based on relationships—not transactions—understanding my clients' goals, and applying my proven, creative expertise to help them.

Business advice: When meeting a client for the first time, don't pontificate about your capabilities before they speak. LISTEN. It's through identifying their needs and goals that you can provide the custom solution they are seeking. Relationships matter, even in the digital era. Why? Because we are human. Interaction builds trust.

Healing lesson: Educate yourself on your diagnosis. Be prepared to ask questions. Communicate your needs. Find the care team that specializes in your illness and embraces you as a person. Interview the medical team as you would to fill a job position. Be your own advocate.

Family

My family is the grounding purpose for all I do, my core value that propelled me to launch my company. Being a hands-on mom for my two daughters was my priority. I did not want to complete an HR form for time off when I wanted to be their classroom mom. I wanted to freely be part of their childhood, creating precious memories. Owning a business provided that flexibility.

Business advice: A wise life force advised that I have one time around as a mom and the years pass quickly. Savor the time. Attend every event. You and your kids will remember what event you missed, but you won't remember the project that kept you from attending! So true! I may have been the last mom in line at pick-up or the last one to enter the auditorium, but I MADE IT!

Healing lesson: Speaking your feelings with family and friends is therapeutic and allows for a supportive environment. Be accepting of help and embrace the power of love. Learn to get in touch with yourself by meditating, which invites healing energy.

Faith

Sprouting from family is faith. Every decision I make is encompassed with faith: faith in God to guide, provide, and protect; faith in myself to believe in my capabilities, to empower myself to achieve even more, and to know I'm worthy of success.

Business advice: Our minds, when in a positive mindset, are more powerful than the limiting conditionings that society and circumstances have taught us to believe. When empowered, creativity and intuition abound, helping us to manifest our dreams.

Healing lesson: Embrace and believe in the power of your inner self. We are far more capable of healing ourselves than Western medicine allows us to believe. Good nutrition, mediation, and prayer are windows to your inner self, God, and the ability to overcome.

Perseverance and Resiliency

According to *Forbes Magazine*, "Eight out of 10 businesses fail in the first 18 months due to lack of persistence." Perseverance is an absolute necessity for success! This attribute is the energy source to sustain your core reason for launching your business and is fueled by the faith you need to grow your business. When a sales seed sprouts with an interested prospect, you immediately cultivate that relationship. Stay in touch with emails, leave a friendly voicemail, or ship a small gift. Why? So, YOU are at the top of the mind when a decision needs to be made.

Business advice: Focusing on your core values will empower you to persevere. You need to find your truth, the real reason why you want to own a business. There's a greater cause that supersedes money only. Define your unique selling proposition and consistently deliver what you promise.

Healing lesson: Do not allow the "what ifs" to overpower your confidence or enthusiasm. Do not allow any diagnosis or statistic to define you. Be resilient—cultivate an attitude of survivorship, find a different perspective in adversity, and quickly rebound.

Intuitiveness

Once you begin your business path, divine coincidences will appear. These "Godwinks" reinforce that you are following the right path. It's that gut feeling, the voice, that extra beat in your heart—all relevant to growing you and your business. Embrace these moments. Do not disregard their meaning.

My example: I was parking for a luncheon in Pittsburgh, but the "voice" guided me to the garage further away, where I ran into a business colleague who shared a referral. That referral turned into a client for five years. For real!

Business advice: Building a referral network is crucial to growing your business. Whether you are on Zoom or in-person, attending events is imperative to building relationships and credibility. I built my agency by attending networking events, charity benefits, and business expos. My advice: SHOW UP AND FOLLOW UP.

Healing lesson: Follow your instincts. Do not allow any medical practitioner to dismiss your feelings or symptoms. Build your network of care providers to encompass the healing of your body, mind, and spirit. Make time to connect with prayer.

Own YOU

Entrepreneurship takes a lot of energy. My friends call me the Energizer Bunny; I have an abundance of energy which I believe is partially genetic and partially derived from truly loving what I do. I am confident in who I am, and I always creatively deliver what I promise for my clients' success.

My example: At a small diverse business luncheon, I approached a buyer from a prominent corporation and pitched my qualified background, to which he replied, "Yeah, I have many people that provide what you do." As I felt my body practically ignite, I calmly rebutted, "I respectfully disagree. My agency is the ONLY outsourced certified women-owned business in this field, covering all of Pennsylvania. Our tactics quantifiably contribute to revenue growth." He offered his card. Be bold! Brag! Own it! Three years I persevered with this corporation. Finally, I procured a contract!

Business advice: Be ready to deliver a message of confidence when you meet a prospect. Create a personal brand that gets you noticed which creates a memorable impression. Add personal touches to client engagements that communicate your authenticity.

Healing lesson: My personal brand statement is my very fashionable shoes. At each chemo session, I rocked my hospital visit wearing trendy footwear. The symbolism? To kick ass! Own your personal brand.

138

Positive Vibes

In November 2020, to express my joy and gratitude, I launched an energizing website and inspirational gift line, I Chose Happy! I want my internal joy and positive vibe to shine outward. I want to inspire people to choose happiness, to find the ray of sunshine in every situation, to know that dreams can be realized even during adversity, like cancer or COVID.

The pandemic environment has caused so much uncertainty, affecting each one of us differently. Ironically, for me, I perceived quarantining in 2020 as a blessing. While continuing treatments, I experienced less stress because there was no work travel or in-person meetings where I could possibly contract an illness. While COVID negatively impacted my business, the happy outcome was I found time to create my positive website which has been in my heart for a long time. As a pay-it-forward in 2021 and beyond, I want to help nonprofits promote their mission by raising money through my customizable inspirational gift line. I also envision corporations co-branding with my inspirational messages and gifts to empower their employees.

Until now, very few people knew of my cancer journey. I was not public with my illness mainly because I am an entrepreneur, responsible for the viability of my agency, fearful that prospects or clients may not engage my services for concerns about long-term viability or ability to meet deadlines. Also, I did not want to burden friends or extended family.

Twenty Won

Fear is burdensome. I've relinquished fear and have personally redefined its meaning. FEAR to me means, "Feel Everything, All Relates." There's a purpose in my journey, all our journeys. Our hearts need to be opened to the lessons we're supposed to learn for fulfillment of our soul, to help others, and to improve our earthly lives. God has sent affirmations that it's time to share my story to help others. I truly hope I have inspired you to take that leap, to embrace your true passion and purpose.

Blessed to outshine the odds in business and cancer, my advice to you: Have faith in God. Believe in YOU. Always persevere. Be resilient. Most of all, CHOOSE HAPPY! This empowering combination will propel you to personal fulfillment and business success!!!

Bio

**Photo by Kara Himich
Photography**

Trendsetter momtrepreneur Maria Theresa gathered her nerve, banking experience, and growing family in 1996 and took a leap of faith. She launched a dynamic marketing agency specializing in financial institution marketing. Keeping her family at the heart of her new business, Marakae Marketing (Ma [short â], Ra [long A], Kae [long A]) fuses the first syllables of Maria's name with those of her daughters, Rachael and Kailey.

Embracing her knowledge, unique creativity, and strong communication skills, several health-care companies, law firms, and universities joined Marakae's client portfolio. Her nationally certified Women Business Entity provides services for branding, consulting, and design along with imprinted corporate gifts and apparel.

Maria's authentic approach with clients and perseverance earned Marakae Marketing a seat in the top 25% of U.S. businesses celebrating 25 years*. She has been featured in local and national publications for her creativity.

Infusing positivity into 2020 and beyond, Maria's intuition spoke to her to launch an inspirational website and gift-line, IChoseHappy.Live. Along with motivational messages, the site ignites positive energy by partnering with local charities for customizable, fundraising gifts. I Chose Happy! is already receiving national attention for creativity and content.

In addition to enjoying her rewarding career, Maria loves to live healthy, cook, garden, and travel. Her extended fur family includes four rescue cats, one dog, and a chinchilla. Maria's happiest moments are when her home is filled with the bustle of family, but mostly the giggles of her grandson, William.

*US Bureau of Statistics.

Connect with Maria

www.ichosehappy.live
www.marakae.biz
Email: maria@marakae.biz
LinkedIn: www.linkedin.com/in/mariatbrady

Leap of Faith

Elizabeth (Li) Connolly

My name is Elizabeth (Li) Connolly, and I am the proud owner of Connolly Steele + Company, a full-service CPA firm located in the North Hills of Pittsburgh. We just celebrated a big milestone, 25 years in business on January 1, 2021.

The existential theologian Paul Tillich wrote that "doubt is not the opposite of faith: it is one element of faith." I believe that in all entrepreneurs there is a small voice of doubt and a giant leap of faith. I like to tell people that being an entrepreneur is a bit like sleeping without a pillow; you are never truly comfortable. But the courage to step out in faith, to grasp the dream of service to others in some way, and to better your own life and those you care about is a common thread that binds entrepreneurs together.

My grandfather ran a successful construction company in Nashville. He was completely intertwined with all the people in his company, from the Board of Directors to the office workers to all the people who worked out on the job sites. He was my first introduction to how to do business right. He made sure that he knew their names and let them know how important each was to him and the success of the company. He treated everyone with respect.

My father, Lewis Jr., was cut from the same cloth. A true renaissance man, he is knowledgeable in matters of philosophy, religion, and how to get around in almost any city. I have the great privilege of working with my father and my husband who runs the IT division of our company. While I learned about what was possible from these men, I also learned that, as a woman, I could be the one to lead.

After graduating in three and a half years from Duquesne University, I started my career at Touche Ross (then one of the "Big 8" accounting firms). I was in the auditing department and enjoyed working on audits of the smaller clients. One of the challenges of working in such a large company was the competitive atmosphere. No matter when I got to work, someone was there before me, and no matter what time I left, there was always someone still working. It felt like no matter how much I gave it just wasn't enough. I told myself that if I ever got to control my own situation, no one who worked for me would ever feel like that. This experience allowed me to overcome my own doubts and set a mission to be inclusive, interconnected, and collaborative.

I enjoyed the camaraderie of working at a big firm where lasting friendships were forged, many of which continue to this day. I got married to my best friend, Mike, who was a Duquesne graduate and an alum of our co-ed business fraternity, Delta Sigma Pi. During those early years with me working at Touche Ross and Mike at Mellon Bank, we traveled quite a bit. I wanted more control over my life as we wanted to start our family.

After almost three years at Touche Ross, I started looking for another job and landed as the first controller at Longue Vue Club. That was a great training ground for me as a place to learn about human resources, budgeting, reporting to a board of directors, and coordinating many department heads. During my time at Longue Vue, my father started working on his own again after many years as a partner with another North Hills firm. He moved his office to the Lawyers Building downtown and commuted to work with my mother who still, after 50 years, works as a professor at Duquesne. He was happy on his own, but it was soon apparent to me that he needed help.

However, his CPA practice was primarily tax-based, and my public accounting experience was in auditing. He has always been a great teacher and showed me the nuances of tax where most policies are illogical. I gave my one-year notice at Longue Vue and worked half time there training my successor while taking the leap of faith to work as an entrepreneur with my father.

During that year, we formed Connolly, Steele & Company, P.C. and launched on January 1, 1996. By that time, I was pregnant with our first son. I knew that I wanted to control my destiny and work for the good of the clients but also to have the flexibility to be the kind of mom I wanted to be. In the beginning, Connolly Steele was a firm of only three, Lewis Steele, Li Connolly (father/daughter duo), and Debbie Merklin (the first + Company). Debbie, who had worked for my father earlier in his time as a sole proprietor, came back to join the father/daughter duo, and we continued to grow from there.

Over the years, we moved from the Lawyers Building back to Ben Avon, just next door to where I had ruled down ledgers many years before. We stayed there for 14 years, expanding our business while adding team members, clients, and capabilities.

Another happy but scary leap of faith was in 2005, when we decided Mike would leave his job in information technology, complete with all the nice, comfortable corporate benefits, to add an IT division to the company. At that point, we had three young sons, keeping us very active in the Cub Scout community while trying to balance our family life with caring for our clients.

My father has always said that I was the boss of him from the time I was born. We did transition the business to be solely mine in terms of ownership. When I first started in public accounting, it was still very much a man's world. But women have caught up in terms of our place in this industry.

My business can be very stressful, with many people looking to us for guidance and answers to questions that they didn't even know to ask. Still, we have a deep, abiding care for our clients, many of whom have been with us for many years. It is important for us to be there and be the steady hand when life gets complicated. That is exactly how we felt in March 2020.

My birthday is March 6th, which is a terrible time to have a birthday if you are a CPA with a concentration in tax matters. I distinctly remember going to a lovely birthday dinner on March 5th, 2020 with my parents, husband, and the two sons who live close by. There had been rumblings about COVID-19, but we still felt very removed from it in Pittsburgh.

During the next week, everything fell apart. By March 13th, Governor Wolf had shut down the state, and only essential businesses could remain open. For one weekend, we were shut down, wondering how we were going to be able to process payroll for our business clients.

But as a business owner, I had to make sure that I was keeping my team safe from this unknown threat. There was so much we didn't know then. How was it transmitted? What about all the paper documents we receive through the mail and those dropped off by clients? What about all the in-person appointments already on the calendar?

How would this affect our staffing? I sent home the two college interns who had been with us since January. I just couldn't bear the responsibility of this threat to these two young women, excited to build some great resume-building experience.

How would this affect our clients? Would my small business clients make it, being forced to shut down? Would they be able to pay our fees? I am in the unique position of being a small business owner who serves many small business owners. We were all in this same, frightening boat. The main difference though was that our clients would need us—their trusted business advisor—now more than ever. I made the decision that we could not panic. Our clients would need us to be the calm in the storm, to help them as we always do, to navigate the uncharted waters that lay ahead.

After the passage of the CARES act on March 27, 2020, we were all scrambling to try and understand this huge law complete with many new acronyms, PPP (Payroll Protection Act) and PUA (Pandemic Unemployment Assistance) among some of the most significant. We were deep into tax season, and April 15th was just around the corner. How would we manage to wrap up all the deadlines, keep ourselves physically safe, and gain a thorough understanding of the significant changes brought about by the CARES act? I knew that it wasn't efficient for all the team to try and be experts in all these matters. We tapped one of our amazing CPAs and tasked her with being the point person on all things COVID relief-related. We sent out many email blasts to keep our clients informed about the ever-changing rules on applying for the relief funds and the appropriate use of those funds. We stayed up to date on the changes on a firm level, but the deep dive was left to one. The rest of the CPA team took on her other client work so she could stay focused on this one area.

The challenges of 2020 continued through the year. All the deadlines were moved to July 15, 2020. Normally, we get a break from the ridiculousness of our life defined by tax season in the first four months of the year where 60% of the work gets done. Now, the initial crunch would be stretched out three additional months. Clients, who were used to the timeline, now had to be reassured at every turn. There were ongoing frustrations with the ever-changing rules of the appropriate use of the PPP funds, applying for small business grants for our clients, and just staying abreast of the interpretations from

Federal and State governments on the tax treatment of the various programs available to help businesses and individuals.

We like to prepare our clients appropriately for the tax consequences of each year and spend much of our time in the fall doing tax planning for our clients. But in the fall of 2020, decisions were made about when and how to spend money based on a set of rules that changed on December 27, 2020. That day, a new tax law, The Consolidated Appropriations Act, 2021, H.R. 133, significantly changed the game and re-introduced some new acronyms like ERC (Employee Retention Credit) previously not available to everyone. It is a reminder that we are needed now more than ever to learn the laws so that we can help understand the impact to our clients and guide them through this most challenging time. I said that the 2020 tax season was the most difficult, but I am feeling that that was just a dress rehearsal for 2021.

I am so proud of the way we rose to the occasion to be there for our clients, to be kind, compassionate, and professional in dealing with the challenges of 2020. If you are human, you have been impacted by the pandemic. We are all doing the best we can and need to recognize the need to remain flexible and nimble in our efforts going forward. When we focus on our guiding principle of service to others, we can all rise together.

I look toward the future with hope while keeping an eye to the past to help remind us that in all things, if done with care and concern, we can continue to be there for our clients. We will support them in their financial journey while maintaining an environment that supports the team who make it all possible. The small voice of doubt will always be there, but the faith that

Twenty Won

our work in service to others matters will support those who make leaps of their own.

Bio

Photo by Lucia Cintra

As the founder and president of Connolly Steele, Li's primary duty is to "run our company to ensure our clients can run theirs." For nearly three decades, she has been helping individuals and businesses make sense of their finances and supporting them in reaching their goals.

Before starting her own firm, Li worked for several years in the auditing department of Touche Ross and was controller at Longue Vue Club. "Opening Connolly Steele was an opportunity for me to help other businesses while being a business owner myself," she says. Family has always been at the center of Connolly Steele: Li's father, Lewis, is a founding principal of the firm; her husband, Mike, runs the technology division; and all of Li's children have spent time working there.

Both Li and her husband are graduates of Duquesne University. They have been married for over 30 years and have three adult children. When they're not hard at work, they enjoy spending time in nature or at home with their cat, Socks.

Twenty Won

Connect with Li

www.connollysteele.com

Growth

Twenty Won

Turning the Pain of Grief into Positive Growth

Elly Sheykhet

The year 2020 was difficult and challenging for everyone. The pandemic has affected every single family in every country while destroying and altering many businesses all around the world. People have suffered losses and been overwhelmed with fear, anxiety, and desperation. It seemed the whole world was falling apart, and everyone was seeking the answer to the same question, "How can I survive this world disaster?"

I was not asking that, though. My own world had already collapsed. I had already experienced the feeling of pandemic when I lost my daughter three years ago. I knew if I could survive my child's murder, then I would be able to handle any other situation in life, no matter how tough and challenging it would be. I did not fear COVID; I have taken advantage of it. As the world slowed down, I was able to pick up all my broken pieces and started moving again, resonating with the slower rhythm of the world.

When I found my daughter's breathless body in 2017, I did not think I could survive. In the blink of an eye, my whole being was shattered into a million pieces, and my life turned into ruins. The loss of a child may be the worst trauma a human being can experience. As a mother I have experienced the greatest pain that any parent can endure. I lost my identity, my faith, and my life purpose. I lost all that I had looked forward to in our future. By losing my daughter, I had lost my entire self.

Going through the grieving process was the most challenging experience of my life. I came face to face with an intense wave of depression; I felt as if I were drowning. I looked into the scary eyes of darkness, those mesmerizing eyes that stare deeply into the eyes of your soul and kindly welcome you to slowly walk down the evil realm further and further until you see the end—where pain and suffering do not exist. I was a step away from it. Yes, I welcomed the suicidal thoughts into my mind. Every night I went to bed and prayed that I would not wake up.

I have felt every single emotion that normally comes with grief: Anger. Shame. Devastation. Depression. Disappointment. Madness. Anxiety. Emptiness. Confusion. Guilt. Hatred. Revenge. And so many other ugly feelings that consumed every cell of my being. At first, those feelings drained my body physically and emotionally, making me dysfunctional to the point where all I could do was blink. I did not have energy for anything else. Then somehow, I picked up all the tiny pieces of my shattered self and started moving forward, carrying those ugly feelings inside.

All those feelings were intense. They drove me insane, filling me with a strong negative power. Managing those forceful, unpleasant energies—especially the overwhelming feelings of hatred toward the person who had deliberately taken my daughter's life away—was challenging. He stole my child's beautiful life filled with love and joy and the promising bright future of my family.

Acknowledging such an unimaginable reality created so much anger in me. I was never that angry in my life. A longing for revenge filled me with the desire to tear the world apart. My ego could not stop that negative force of power, but my soul— my bleeding, tortured soul—has found a solution for survival. With God's help, I realized that I could use that power for my own soul's benefit. It took a lot of courage and hard work, but I transformed the power of pain into the power of love.

We grieve the loss of our loved ones deeply when our love is great, but we suffer because our love has no place to go. We grieve because we cannot express our love to those who are no longer physically here. With God's help, I learned how to express my love to my daughter through my passions. In two years, I learned how to use my grief as a tool for my creativity. The more pain I felt, the more creative I became. I could do things I was never capable of. That is how Alina's Light was born.

Alina's Light is a nonprofit charitable organization founded in memory of my daughter Alina, who was an exceptional young woman. She radiated love, life, and energy. She had a compassionate spirit that made everyone around her feel special. In her short twenty years, she lived more life than some people who are in their eighties. I knew my daughter's death was not in vain; such a bright and beautiful life had to be honored in many ways.

Alina's Light became my child. Running an organization that is so close to my heart brings me sanity. Our organization focuses on helping others who share Alina's passions. To honor her enormous love for children and animals, we make continuing donations to children's hospitals and animal shelters. Alina was a talented performer who loved singing and dancing. To honor her passion for musical theater, Alina's Light provides scholarships to the seniors of her high school who perform at the school musicals. Also, we provide support to women and their children who are in abusive relationships, and we make donations to numerous women's shelters. Alina's Light has built a close relationship with The Women's Center and Shelter of Pittsburgh. Our team visits the facility during the holidays, organizing parties and providing residents with holiday gifts. Honoring Alina's legacy by raising awareness and promoting domestic violence education are at the core of Alina's Light's mission.

Right before the pandemic started, our team had presented our first lecture to educate young men and women about the danger of dating violence. Alina's Light had the honor of bringing Alina's story to her high school at the 2020 Winter Jamfest to End Domestic Violence basketball tournament where we held five presentations that day for a total of ten teams from different states. Before each game, the two teams that were playing gathered in a conference room to listen to our lecture. One of our board members shared the statistics and red flags of domestic violence along with the importance of recognizing those signs and taking necessary actions to either stop your own toxic relationships or help others get out of abusive relationships.

Though the young men were paying attention to this sensitive topic, I noticed that they still whispered with each other and fidgeted in their seats. However, when Alina's picture was displayed as a face of domestic violence and I, a mother of a domestic violence victim, stepped in to present, their jaws dropped, and silence filled the room.

I shared Alina's story and how I found her the day she passed. I delivered my personal message about the danger of domestic violence and how important it is to break the silence on this global issue. Throughout my presentation, the audience unblinkingly stared at me. I felt emotional sharing some details of Alina's story, but realizing how important that message was gave me strength to ground myself. With no doubt, I felt that my words were heard and made an impact on their lives. That day made a huge shift in my grieving process. I felt as if my soul's purpose was calling; I knew it was my mission now to share Alina's story and save others' lives.

The year 2020 was supposed to be a productive and growing year for our organization. Even though my husband and I were still overwhelmed by grief, we looked forward to having a few events. Our second annual Alina's Light Run and Walk for Love event was scheduled in July as a celebration of Alina's birthday. The first event, in 2019, was a beautiful celebration and huge success—we raised tens of thousands of dollars. Six hundred people gathered to celebrate Alina's life and bring awareness to domestic violence. It was a family-oriented event with different activities for all ages. We had food trucks, ice cream stations, live bands, a petting zoo, crafts for kids, and yoga and massages for adults. A local dance school that was Alina's second home brought their dancers to perform at the event in honor of Alina. At the end of the day, we released a few beautiful doves for Alina's birthday. We projected 2020's event to be an even bigger success, but unfortunately, due to the pandemic, all our events—like many of the other events in the world—were cancelled. And like many other organizations around the world, we took the opportunity to explore alternatives.

In October, domestic violence awareness month, we were supposed to have another annual event—a Tackle Domestic Violence football game. Instead, we had a virtual concert broadcasted live over Zoom. We provided our supporters with a beautiful night of live entertainment, raffles, and virtual fun that reminded them of how crucial it is to be neighborly and kind amidst the chaos.

Despite all the hardships of the pandemic, Alina's Light has made a significant impact in 2020 in Alina's memory. From hospitals, to domestic violence shelters, to animal shelters, to homeless shelters, to food banks, we have proudly spread our light to thousands in our community.

Alina's Light has been fighting for change since day one. We are working hard to get Alina's Law passed. Alina's Law, PA House Bill 588, aims to strengthen protection from abuse orders (PFAs), transforming them from a mere piece of paper to a lifesaving option for victims of domestic violence. In the beginning of 2020, Alina's Light, accompanied by our families and friends, traveled to Harrisburg to support state representative Anita Kulik as she presented the bill. I spoke to the crowd inside the Pennsylvania State Capitol to stress the importance of Alina's Law and why it needs to be passed. We do everything in our power to keep fighting and hope to get the law passed.

COVID has stopped some of our projects for now, though. Alina's Dolls, a permanent public art installation designed as a powerful memorial for victims of domestic violence, is one of them. Alina's Dolls would create a perfect space for support, companionship, meditation, and healing through hands-on doll making and doll decorating. We are counting on support of the city government officials to bring this project to the public.

Taking advantage of extra free time during the pandemic, I have finished and published my book One Year After to support other grieving parents and give them hope. Also, I have finished a few mediumship and energy healing courses and have been inspiring others by providing spiritual guidance and support.

My biggest challenge in 2020 was missing my daughter's physical presence, but her energy, her spirit, her guidance, and her support from the higher realm are always here. Going through such a challenging year made our bond and our connection even stronger. She taught me to light a candle instead of cursing the darkness. I finished a From Grief to

Gratitude Coach Certification program and became a certified grief coach. My mission and passion now are to guide and empower others. Alina's Light Grief Coaching sessions are available for those who try to navigate this difficult journey and want to find hope, achieve growth, and maintain gratitude throughout life.

The year 2020 was challenging for everyone. It tested our strength and perseverance. Everyone has experienced some type of loss due to the pandemic—a job, a marriage, a friendship, a loved one. We all are human beings, so we all experience loss at some point in life. We all go through challenges and suffer. I truly believe that, when we suffer, we activate our God-given power. But it is up to us how we use it. You can decide which direction to let that power go. You have two choices: You either keep it as a power of pain and destroy yourself and everything around you, OR you transform it into the power of love and create beautiful things.

Though I experienced the greatest loss in life, I decided to take my suffering as a gift and use it for making this world a better place.. And if I could do it, you can do it too. Let the pain direct your life, not ruin your life. Use the power of pain to transform you into your best self.

Bio

Photo by Archie Carpenter

Elly Sheykhet was born in Ivanovo, Russia, and spent her childhood alongside her parents and two brothers. After finding love and getting married, Elly moved to the United States in 2000 with her husband, Yan, and two beautiful children, Artem and Alina. In 2003, Elly obtained her associate's degree in accounting at Pittsburgh's ICM School of Business. Also, Elly holds a master's degree in economics that she earned in Russia and validated in the United States.

She is currently employed at Henderson Brothers, an insurance agency in downtown Pittsburgh and serves as their accountant and cash manager. After losing her 20-year-old daughter, Alina, in a senseless act of violence in 2017, Elly and her husband founded Alina's Light, a nonprofit organization established in her memory. This organization is very dear to the Sheykhets and is often referred to by Elly as "her child." The mission of Alina's Light, among others, is to give voice to the victims of domestic violence through the arts, community events, and charitable actions.

Elly is a published author and serves as a certified grief coach; she has dedicated her life to honoring her daughter by helping others. She hopes to brighten the world in Alina's memory.

Twenty Won

Elly cherishes the time she spends with family and is a proud grandmother to Artem's daughter, Angelina.

Connect with Elly

elly.sheykhet@alinaslight.com
www.alinaslight.com/
www.facebook.com/alinaslight
www.instagram.com/alinaslight_/
Book: www.amazon.com/Elly-Sheykhet/e/B088DKD551?

A Servant's Heart

Suzanna Masartis

I once read that "whoever wants to be great must become a servant." In the nonprofit world, we choose to serve others. Perhaps that is the reason nonprofits can be so successful—the drive to serve is more than a job; it is a passion! I have been serving in the nonprofit world for 31 years. Today, I lead the Community Liver Alliance (CLA), and I feel fortunate to do so. The CLA is a nonprofit, community-based organization dedicated to promoting liver health and liver disease awareness, prevention, education, advocacy, and research. Supported by a network of patients, caregivers, health care professionals, and community leaders, the organization develops and runs educational workshops; provides expertise and leadership for statewide viral hepatitis elimination plans; conducts screenings; coordinates support groups; facilitates linkage to necessary medical care; provides education for policy makers on issues related to liver health; and works with community leaders and groups to raise awareness about liver disease.

Twenty Won

Members of the CLA, including the Father of Transplantation, Dr. Thomas E. Starzl, were a part of a national liver nonprofit organization for more than a decade. In 2013 we seceded to create the CLA with the idea to do something different, better even, by providing the community with tangible services and support to patients; meaningful education for providers, patients, and the community; true advocacy initiatives that inspire positive change; and a nimble response to the ever-changing liver space.

It was a bold idea by a patient's mom, Joanne, who was determined and fearless in her endeavor. She gathered a committed and passionate group of doctors, nurses, patients, and friends to have a meeting at the Panera in Oakland, Pa., to ask for their help. It was a profound effort by these amazing volunteer leaders to join forces and create the CLA. I was and still am very grateful that they brought me along!

We quickly achieved our local goals and began growing across the nation to address the same issues that we faced in Pennsylvania. Our growth has been deliberate yet organic as our work has expanded. We forged a path in central Appalachia where there is always a great need and very little resources. Meanwhile, our work in disparate and marginalized communities has been the most rewarding.

As a lifelong servant, I am grateful for the journey that brought me here—to the exact place where I am supposed to be—and I am grateful for the opportunity to share it.

My journey as a servant started as a teenager as part of my church's Christian Youth Organization. I joined because my other friends were a part of it, and we had fun volunteering at the local rehabilitation center and participating in the church bake sales. Volunteering is what would ignite my true passion as a nonprofit leader.

I had a plan for my life. I thought I would finish high school, go to college, and move to the West Coast. As they say, life had plans for me: I finished high school, started college, fell in love, and had a child very young. I like to describe it as boarding a plane to Paris and finding yourself in Italy; it is an equally beautiful and amazing journey, and I can't imagine my life any other way. I was the youngest stay-at-home mom in the neighborhood. As my friends were graduating college and starting new careers, I joined the local Welcome Wagon to meet other stay-at-home mothers and immediately found myself leading the Ways and Means Committee. I really felt so "grown up" among those amazing, supportive women. I planned my first real fundraiser—a Night at the Races held at the Holiday Park Fire Hall. It was a great time, but we actually lost money—Oops!

Volunteering filled my life with purpose outside of my family even though my family joined me often to help with events. I loved volunteering in the town where I grew up because it gave me the opportunity to be with old and new friends who had a heart for giving back to our community. Soon, I was invited by another member of the Welcome Wagon to join a group who wanted to start the first library. I immediately said "YES!" and served on the Board of Directors to lead the fundraising activities. We had fun, planning and executing a variety of events. We raised a lot of money and gathered local government support to rent a small space and eventually to hire a librarian. Many other awesome volunteers came after us, and the library has become one of the jewels in the crown of Plum Borough, as well as a jewel in my career of which I am very proud.

Recognizing that I needed more than my current job as an administrative assistant, but unable to risk a bold move yet, I started a home-based company called Every Event. I remember sitting around the dining room table with my sister and husband to develop our vision, values, and mission. I worked full-time while we ran the company on the side. We helped local and national nonprofit organizations plan fundraising events. It was the first time I was doing what I really loved, the first time I turned my lifelong love of serving into a paid opportunity. Eventually, I transitioned from my full-time job to focus on my passion.

I did not realize at the time that I was an "entrepreneur." I DO remember enjoying (for the FIRST time) the ability to determine my destiny. It was also a scary time because the reality was that I had to make enough money to contribute to the family household. I would often lie awake at night wondering how I was going to sustain the business, it being a "roll up your sleeves and make it happen" situation. I created my own brochures to send to potential clients via snail mail, and one brochure resulted in an invitation to pitch a Casino Night to the local Chamber of Commerce. I had my proposal ready in a snazzy folder, and my fee was set in stone. I left the meeting with half of the fee, a free membership to the Chamber of Commerce, and eventually a seat on their Board of Directors. We even made money this time. I still think of this as a win because it led to many other opportunities and provided experience in the art of negotiation.

Don't forget this was the mid-1980s—before the internet! I bought a Compaq computer, had a dot matrix printer, and went to the library— yes, that one we raised money to build— to research books for information on themes of the events I was creating. I would make copies of pages to know what colors and details would help me to develop a successful Mardi Gras party. To find potential clients, I scoured the Yellow Pages. I would think in themes—all the chambers of commerce, the area country clubs, youth sports teams. I would pick up the phone, learn the correct contact, have a conversation, and, hopefully, schedule a meeting. I came across those dusty files in my attic with the now-yellowed 10-cent copied pages tucked inside. It brought a smile to my face and sweet memories of a time that seems so long ago.

I enjoyed every aspect of the work then, and I still do today— from researching potential clients, funders, volunteer leaders, and allies to forging strong relationships. What I realize is that the foundation of either side of nonprofit development never changes. It is the passion you bring to one event or cause—or even decade—that creates success. You have to LOVE what you do!

A pivotal organization that helped to form my nonprofit career was the Dollar Energy Fund which I joined as a full-time staff member after consulting for three months. I love the mission and the grassroots work Cindy, the executive director, set forth to create an amazing legacy. Cindy is a true mentor of mine as she led by example. I was fascinated by her ability to form strong partnerships, quickly assess a situation, understand the opportunity, and then make it happen! She took a Pittsburgh-based organization and expanded the services and programs across the nation. She was unconventional, honest, and had a servant's heart towards the mission to help those in great need. Her inspiration to me is unmatched.

As I am called to remember my journey, I'm reminded how necessary journeys are for success. It's true when they say success doesn't happen overnight. I always knew that I was to serve my community—from the library to the CLA. But it's with the memories that I can truly acknowledge: I am where I am today because it is exactly where I am supposed to be.

If you've achieved success, you know what it means to pivot and turn. Nonprofits know this all too well, even during "normal" times. Our most recent success and national expansion happened in 2020 during the pandemic—a year for the history books. I was in North Carolina presenting at a National Harm Reduction Conference when the world began to realize we were in trouble. I arrived at the airport to travel home, and the vibe was ominous. I remember thinking, "This is really bad"—we didn't realize how bad it was going to get.

When I arrived at the office on Monday, I met with our staff and began to plan, but we honestly didn't know what we were planning for. Everything was unknown, and it was already a tumultuous time in our country with the racial unrest and bleak political landscape. We tried to approach the situation with a positive attitude that this would all blow over by summer. As it evolved, it became very clear that this was not going to go away anytime soon.

We are a small but mighty organization, yet we didn't have the infrastructure to stay in it for the long haul. If we were going to survive, we had to think outside of our current business model. We recognized we had to invest in initiatives that were going to bring the most value to our liver community and reap the best financial reward. We also realized that we needed to seek an outside consultant to help us develop a winning strategy. I believe things happen the way they are supposed to or that what you put out into the world comes back to you. Whatever you call it, not a day later, I received an email that one of our funders had a special by-invitation-only capacity building grant to help current grantees during the pandemic. And I just knew it was meant to be. We drafted a strong and compelling proposal, which got funded, and we hired our consultant to begin mapping our new direction.

Our reputation and commitment opened doors that may have not otherwise been opened. We led with our mission which set us apart from the rest. While we spent many years collectively in the liver space as advocates, providers, patients, and caregivers, we did not realize what we really had until we had to have IT. Our ability to be nimble and creative allowed us to pivot when the pandemic happened. We embraced the need to change, but we thrived because we were ready to serve.

We keep our expenses low and have a board-designated reserve. When hard times hit, we were steadfast. Our mindfulness of keeping within our budget and investing in expertise—like our strategic planning consultant—as we needed it allowed us to cobble together strong, effective teams to move our mission forward.

Twenty Won

Raising more money in 2020 than we had ever raised before despite the pandemic, we continued to provide meaningful education, held two fun "virtual" events, and funded our annual research grant. We were able to accomplish this because we have grown to really know the community and learned the value of relationships, what is relevant in our domain, and how to be responsive and resilient.

During this growth, I was able to hire former colleagues with whom I worked at previous nonprofit organizations to help us push through and plan for the future. I believe we will continue to find success because of our visionary Board of Directors and our amazing staff.

Drawing from our experience and what we learned from other organizations we worked for and with, we especially understood what works and, more importantly, what doesn't work—because we've been there. We know and embrace the concept of "if you want something other than what you have, you must do something you've never done before." The model we now have allows us to embrace technology to reach a greater number of those we serve.

Above all else, we embraced the uniqueness of working in the nonprofit sector. The drive to serve is as great as the drive to be successful. It's a powerful combination that compelled us even during the darkest hours.

Our journey during a global pandemic has certainly been a wild ride, and it is not over. We've learned much last year, and we are as prepared for 2021 as we can be. As a health organization, we are still embracing technology for a contactless year of events and programs. Leading with our mission to host many more programs than we will fundraising events, we continue to develop our strategic plan and remain nimble to navigate these uncertain days. We will also remain positive that things will get better soon.

We remain positive because it is our time in liver treatment—with a cure for hepatitis C and new therapies for other liver diseases which we never had before. It is with pride that I recognize CLA is a legacy which will exist and continue to serve the liver community long after I am gone. But in the meantime, I am looking forward to what comes next after the pandemic.

Bio

Photo by Stephanie Laura Photography

Suzanna is a consummate professional whose career spans more than 25 years of progressive, nonprofit experience. Suzanna has worked as the director of development for the Dollar Energy Fund, as corporate development officer for the American Cancer Society, and as the executive director for the American Liver Foundation. She currently is the CEO for the Community Liver Alliance.

She has worked extensively in the areas of development, program development and implementation, corporate development, external communications, public relations, social media, community and governmental affairs, advocacy activities, coalition development, strategic planning, event planning, board development, volunteer management, and overall operational strategy.

Over the last two and a half decades, having grown to really know the community and learn the value of relationships, Suzanna is an experienced leader with an impeccable reputation across the nation.

Connect with Suzanna

communityliveralliance.org
Suzanna@communityliveralliance.org

Failure to Launch

Gabrielle Smith Noye

Polymath, Renaissance Woman, Jill of all trades. All these terms mean that you're an interesting sort of character who chose more than one path in life. In clever ways, our self-help culture has created reframes to make the lack of a singular purpose acceptable. Currently, the business ecosystem promotes the value of niching down and specializing. However, the entrepreneurial mind seems to me to be more of a generalist (because you can hire a specialist). There is a certain kind of romanticism associated with being a Renaissance person as the name implies—what could be more romantic than a "renaissance"?

If you have ever felt like a Renaissance woman, did you plan for that, or did it just life simply unfold that way? I came to be a renaissance woman both by accident and by nature. I wanted that singular vision and path. I was born with an abundance of creative energy, fierce curiosity, and restlessness. As you can gather, diverse interests can make long-term planning a challenge. Do I turn left at this fork or right? When multiple things spark curiosity and engage the mind, choosing feels heavy.

Did you know the root meaning of the word "decide" means to cut off? To make a decision you have to kill off another option. Choosing is brutal! And worse, how do we know the pursuit is worthy or if you are overly impressionable? Could it be that the so-called "pivot" that many people take in their personal and professional life is healthy, normal, and an opportunity to embrace maturity and self-actualization?

There was no career or turn-key business waiting for me after I spent years studying subjects, like: yoga, psychology, creativity, coaching, magic, childbirth, and design. My skill set more closely resembled the village witch. I'd be fine with that, except there is little demand, unfortunately. I also did not expect my unorthodox training to provide a solid career path. I was comfortable with experimentation and a level of uncertainty.

Years ago, I tried to make myself a resume, and it was obvious—on paper—how unemployable I really was—even with a job history. (Granted, it is challenging to highlight your own strengths when writing a resume). So, how do you wrap up a package of rainbow hippie skills and tie it up with a professional bow? You get better at branding and marketing yourself.

Paradoxically, I have felt both "ahead of" and "behind" my time my whole life—like an outsider who was struggling to catch up with the big kids and make my mark. But what was the "mark" I wanted to make? After my birth doula work, I wanted to embrace my entrepreneurial spirit. I planned to start a business in creativity coaching. I led mindfulness painting workshops for a few years. But I was too afraid to really go for it. Something was off in my business model. I also got stuck on "how" and "who." I felt like there was something missing (maybe there was, or maybe I made that up due to fear).

Now, several years later, I have two coaching methods under my belt, and I know that I can use those anytime in my work, whether or not I decide to have a coach label. Learning those modalities taught me a lot about myself. It also taught me that coaching is primarily a heart-centered path. And while I am a giver in my personal life, I am more of a creator and visionary in my professional life.

Before the pandemic, I worked in an office building at my nine-to-five job. I spent some of my morning commutes in existential grief. In my heart, I knew I could not do this job forever (even though I'd only been there a year). There was nothing wrong with my job, and I was grateful to have it. Still, I could not shake the feeling that I was squandering something—some gift that I never fully opened and accepted. Today, I know that nothing keeps me from my gifts but me— not my job, not my circumstances, just me.

While working my day job, I also lumbered along in a training program for home staging, though I had lost most of my motivation for that by spring of 2020. I keep reminding myself that I chose home staging and design because it was fun. I had never let myself choose something because it was "fun." It always had to be practical, reasonable, and helpful first. Having said that, I do agree that form follows function.

Could I let myself choose what I really wanted? That is the question that started my 2020 shift. After the shutdown, a friend shared a personal development program with me. After working with the tools, I saw a lot about myself—things I never saw from other programs, courses, seminars, etc. You know you are onto something when you start taking actions you could not take before. In this new space, choosing what I wanted didn't seem impossible, and there was less resistance than before.

Inside this incubation period—which is what I believe 2020 was—I found the growth I needed and a new orientation. I began making goals again. No one hated goals more than me at that point. The idea of goals is great, but my goals were so muddled in "shoulds" and came from a negative vision. A negative vision is one you hold for yourself and try to live up to, but since it is inauthentic and *not yours*, it often feels like an uphill battle that requires an iron-strong will to execute. My vision-worthiness gauge is this: If I need to rely solely on willpower to achieve something, my vision is not mine; it's not true. Shifting my language from "goals" to "true choices" helped me see where my goals were coming from— true vision. I also came to see that my old goals were mostly bullshit—stuff that sounded good, significant, worthy of attention, stuff I *could* do but may not really want to do, much less commit to. My old goals were echoes of a false vision I created for myself. No wonder I wasn't interested.

Twenty Won

Feeling stuck in my house, working from a home-office-bedroom, and seeing my resistance to running a business, I had to ask myself again: "What am I hungry for?"

Why did I have so much trouble launching a business all those years before the COVID era? I ask myself this a lot. I sometimes felt guilt or shame about these failures because I couldn't give myself any credit. It's not like I sat around and had nothing to do all day. I had children to care for, a household to run, and a self-employed husband who needed business support; I was always occupied. And I still wanted my own thing. I won't tell you about all the training I did or the crazy ideas I had that never amounted to anything; it's embarrassing. But I will tell you this: When you get prolific at churning out ideas and leaving them out to breathe as you examine from a distance, you get better at discerning which ones might actually work.

When it came to business ideation, the biggest lesson I had to learn in 2020 is to make what people will *buy*, not what I want to sell them. Simple economics. Sometimes, we get trapped thinking we need to monetize EVERYTHING we are good at. I distrust the common marketing phrase, "Monetize your passion." No, some passions are more fulfilling left as hobbies! We need to bring those back. That is what being a renaissance person is about: having interests that you pursue for the sheer joy of it. No strings attached. Sure, there will be a crossover, but it needs to be a problem people would pay me to solve. My intention is to create an E.L.F business (Easy, Lucrative, Fun); I'm not trying to solve extreme problems in difficult ways with difficult people.

In addition to providing something people would pay for, I noticed there were gaps in education around personal branding, messaging, and launching that were not being addressed, not even by the speaking organization I was affiliated with. From my experience working with women and marketing, a failure to launch often boils down to three things:

Lack of confidence

Lack of focus

Lack of purpose

Every one of those things is affected by the overarching question: How hungry are you? If you are comfortable where you are at, you might not feel that push that others feel when they start a business or movement. When this happens, you let yourself get delayed and derailed—simply because you can afford to. To be hungry is to be a little uncomfortable.

If you are dangerously low in confidence, focus, and/or purpose, launching anything will be like rolling a boulder uphill, naked. This is how it felt for me. There will be so much resistance on your path. So, what do you do? Go work on yourself for dozens of years like I did? Go for perfection first? No. You must start where you are and be willing to do it poorly. That is hard to hear, but we gain confidence by doing. Well, that is one way. There are other ways to help that involve personal coaching at the conscious and the subconscious level. So much of what we do to improve ourselves is in the conscious realm. But there is a lot you can affect under the surface as well, if you have the tools. We are icebergs, and we need to start looking below the surface.

Focus is essential to launching, especially if you have many other things to focus upon or, like me, you give yourself too many things to focus upon. Do yourself a favor and clear your plate as much as possible. Let the unimportant stuff go. Without focus, nothing happens. You can outsource some focus, but ultimately, being able to cultivate focus will serve your highest potential in all areas of life. To increase your focus, begin by retraining your mind to focus on less things. Go deeper, not wider. Lessen your digital distractions, especially. You could also meditate if you do not already. Just sit and do nothing for 10 minutes. It's that easy! I'm kidding; it is not.

Purpose can't be outsourced; you must understand why you do what you do. It doesn't have to be lofty or grand either. Maybe you don't want to make a global impact or solve world hunger. That is fine. You can be purposeful and serve in your own lane, so to speak, wherever that may be. Just do you. That is what ultimately attracts others to you and your business.

The COVID-19 shutdown did a powerful thing for me: It helped me create space. The space to rethink, to reprioritize, and to recreate. As the world slowed down, I felt I could catch my breath and take a time-out. Yes, 2020 was an immense ordeal. For me, 2019, 2014, and 1997 were much worse. You have your years too, I bet; years stricken with illness, divorce, strife, and loss.

If economic chaos, isolation, and a global pandemic isn't a catalyst for personal change, I don't know what is. I used 2020 as my year to let go of what was not working. I started with my mind using conscious and subconscious processes to understand why I was creating what I had been. I didn't do it alone; I had the help of teachers.

As the saying goes, nature abhors a vacuum. As you destroy, you must create. Instead of problem-solving my way through life, I tried something new: moving towards what I love. It was a matter of focus and orientation. When we are fighting problems (or ourselves), we don't have the energy to focus on creating. This Buckminster Fuller quote says this another way: "You never change things by fighting the existing reality. To change something, build a new model that makes the existing model obsolete."

Be fierce in your choosing and go magically in the direction of your dreams—especially if you are a renaissance person who feels paralyzed by indecision and doubt as I did. Accept your funky, unorthodox ways and get on with creating your life.

Bio

Photo by Becky Bickford

Gabrielle is a designer, writer, and visual artist with an entrepreneurial spirit. She has worked in various sectors including community arts, women's health, and marketing. For decades, her journey in the personal development world has dovetailed with her journey in the professional world. She is an advocate of integrating the two worlds within, so we can serve our highest potential. She has also trained with the KaizenMuse creativity method and the Magnetic Mind coach training.

She was born and raised in the Southern California suburbs. Living in various communities over her adult life (from California to Hawai'i to Canada) helped her become agile, observant, and appreciative of diversity. Gabrielle uses her creativity and marketing skills in her staging and design company, Abria Interiors. Her branding and consulting services can be found at www.gabysmithnoye.com.

When she isn't managing multiple passions in her work, she enjoys traveling to wilderness, dancing, and studying subjects like Druidry, physics, and folk medicine. She lives in Western Pennsylvania with her family and cat, Tulsi.

Connect with Gabrielle

Brand Consulting: www.gabysmithnoye.com
Home Staging Services: www.abriainteriors.com
Instagram: @GabySmithNoye

If you have any questions for me or wish to discuss any aspect of my shared story, I am an open book.

Empowerment

Twenty Won

Empower Your Future

Renee DeMichiei Farrow

COVID-19 . . . WHAT?! I wasn't going to let the pandemic stop me from networking or living . . . I stepped into a strange new world, like we all did. I love life, people, working my passion, helping people, and discovering new roads to travel and explore. This was not going to stop me; I would find other ways, and I did.

Ok, I must admit, it scared me. Was I going to lose my full-time job— business development in government, higher ed, retail, and healthcare in the architectural world? How could this be happening? I just returned from a culinary trip to Calabria, Italy, with my husband, friends, and family in January. Most of us got sick there, and when we arrived home via Rome to JFK airport, little did we know our lives would be turned upside down and inside out in a few short weeks.

In early February 2020, before the COVID lockdowns, I restarted my old window treatment company, Decorating Details, to help my children with their new homes and maybe segue into retirement down the road. It was an award-winning and very successful business that I had from 1992 to 2005. I grew it from residential to high-end nursing homes across the US with close to three-quarters of a million dollars in sales and four employees. Why decorating? In 1982 to 1993 I worked part-time in a drapery wholesale company with a drapery workroom and learned that business from top to bottom over 11 years. As you continue with my journey, you will find out how I did pivot and believed in myself. I hope a few of the following tips will resonate with you and your future passion because you just need to do it. It will be an incredible journey for you.

TIP #1

Keep educating and investing in yourself to proliferate your opportunities. In the middle of March, I enrolled in a leadership program, Coro Women in Leadership—an intense program that positions women to become top decision makers at area startups, government agencies, and nonprofits. It was the first cohort at Coro that went totally virtual, which was very complicated. I graduated in July, and our team project was to write a one-time magazine called the "Future is Female" for which each member submitted a story about facing and overcoming a challenge.

Invest in yourself; you are never too young or old to learn new things and continue to be your Best and Ideal Self. I am 62 years old and, going into this pandemic, I invested close to $10,000 to better myself and learn new skills. Not knowing if I would lose my full-time job, it was risky, but the timing was right. Instead of networking and going out four or five nights a week, I had to do something with my time during the lockdown, so why not go for it?

TIP #2

Have fun and expand on something you do well—then run with it. Cooking with Renee DeMichiei Farrow was born as an online Facebook Live cooking show to keep me busy during COVID and help people learn to make and enjoy easy Italian and Slovak dishes. After all there was nothing to do but cook and eat. After doing a few live shows to feel comfortable, I added some Facebook ads to expand my outreach which led to hundreds of views on some of my shows. This is my ethnic heritage, and I tell stories of my family while teaching you to cook. If my parents were alive today, they sure would get a kick out of it, and my dad would be saying, "Mangia!" ("eat" in Italian). My mom's dying wish in 1993 was for me to learn how to make nut rolls. I am so glad I gave in and made them. She is with me always, especially when I am making them. Her sisters told me that mine are the best in the family, and I am now the official nut-roll maker for all the family wedding cookie tables. (It is a Pittsburgh tradition—you must have a cookie table at your wedding!) I plan on doing classes in person as soon as we are able and the virus is gone.

TIP #3

In business, keep your eyes and ears open, and ask questions, no matter where you work. You could start your own business with what you learn. That is how I started Decorating Details. I was working for a wholesale drapery company where I worked my way up from receptionist to marketing to inside and outside sales. Always engaged, asking questions, listening, and just going for it, I developed our first marketing brochure and worked to get our owners on the cover of a national magazine. Who would have known that it would have led to owning my own company that went nationwide? I went from residential design to working on high-end nursing homes across the United States, winning many awards and honors in business including the US SBA Women in Business Advocate Award, the Girl Scout Woman of Distinction Award, the YWCA Tribute to Women Award, and being named one of Pennsylvania's Best 50 Women In Business. My biggest honor was being awarded a Distinguished Alumni from my high school, Plum Borough. Yes, this can be YOU!

TIP #4

It is never too late to start another career. My passion has always been entrepreneurship since opening my first business, and it led me to my next career move working toward my long-awaited retirement years. Duquesne University has a professional coaching program which is one of the top-rated in the country, so I signed up and started another COVID virtual class in August 2020. I will graduate as a certified professional coach in April 2021. Results With Renee Farrow will enable me to help people find their Ideal Self, which will enable them to live their best life, raise their leadership skills, enable executive growth, or help them decide if starting a business is right for them. If I can help someone not make the mistakes I did, it will all be worth it.

TIP #5

Get involved on boards and join organizations. Be a helper, find your passions and what causes you care about, and dig in. Engage by speaking up, offering a helping hand, attending meetings, getting on committees, and eventually running for a board position. Doing all these things will lead to finding new ideas and opportunities, meeting new people, growing your business, and making lifelong friends. Over the years, with Decorating Details, I have had sales over $700,000 and still counting; just by joining, showing up, and getting involved. One last thing . . . I ran for office twice, and I cannot begin to tell you how that impacted my life, my business, and new relationships with powerful people. I was given the opportunity to speak for former Lieutenant Governor, Catherine Baker Knoll, of the State of Pennsylvania, when she was unable to come to Pittsburgh. Imagine that—a little town girl from a coal mining town; and it could be you!

TIP #6

Bring others along, break that glass ceiling. I have always been an advocate for women and minorities all my business life and have won many local and national awards for propelling and advising them to start and grow their businesses. Think of who helped you and what it did for you in your journey. Who have you helped, and what did it do for them? Who are you helping now, and who can you help tomorrow, the next day, week, month, or year? It makes a difference; you will alter their lives. What better way to have a chance to change a life, just by reaching out and mentoring? Please think about transferring your successes by reaching a helping hand and taking them along your journey. I have done this many times; it always gets better and truly makes my life complete.

TIP #7

Honor your commitments, if you say you are going to do it . . . do it. This goes for anything in life: your job, your business, your organizations, boards, your family, your friends. My dad's lifelong message to me and my brothers was to never ever damage your reputation; it's your name also, and it is the only one you will ever have. Make good on your word always; if you say you will do something, follow through. If you run a business and something goes wrong, be the first to make that hard call to explain what went amiss or why there is a delay. It will save you later and keep you from a bad referral.

TIP #8

Go the extra mile, under promise, and over deliver. This is part of the fabric of my being; I always go the extra mile for everyone. If they are sick or having a bad day, I make food, take flowers, or just pick up the phone to let them know I am thinking of them. In my business I learned the hard way. When the blinds are supposed to be in and they do not make it for the holidays or for a special event, you are going to have to explain why. Therefore, you should always under-promise, and when you over-deliver, it goes a long way. Always send a thank-you card or a small gift (especially if they give you a referral), and you will have a customer for life.

TIP #9

ASK for what you want. Asking has been my secret sauce in life. If you do not ask, you will never hear the word YES. Take a minute and really think about how important it is to ask for what you want or need in life and how many times it could have changed your life or the direction it was going. It is too powerful to not put this word (ask) at the top of your thoughts and do it often. I would never be where I am at if I chose not to ask; this is an important lesson that I always discussed with my children. I have so many examples that I could share, but it would cover a whole chapter. It is very important to give someone the chance to say "Yes," so keep in mind just how valuable it is. Also, never, never end a conversation or meeting without asking at the appropriate time.

TIP #10

Get a professional coach! I wanted to end with this very important tip because few people are aware of all a professional coach can do to help you find your Ideal Self, which is who you want to be. Coaches will help you find who you are deep within your being, teach you how to make good choices, and guide you toward new heights. As I enter this new uncharted territory, I know I will always have a coach challenging me to be my Ideal Self. Your Ideal Self is learning how to live your life without the chatter of the inner critic, along with the ability to think outside the box to find the peace and answers you are looking for.

* * *

Twenty Won

As I reflect upon what I wrote in the chapter called "From Coal Town to Uptown" from my 2013 book, *Empower! Women's Stories of Breakthrough, Discovery, and Triumph,* my message still rings true today (2021) and stands the test of time: All leaders face many obstacles and challenges on the path to enjoying triumphant wins. Meanwhile, as entrepreneurs and employees, we all succeed when we have a clear understanding that helping others not only empowers them, but it also empowers ourselves. "Don't stop believing, hold on to that feeling;" you can do whatever you dream to be. And live life, because you only get one.

My word for 2021 is "Pivot," all while stepping into success. My pivot was finding new ways to network at my full-time job and to fill the nights I would have normally spent going out to events and dinners by doing a few new things. Summing it up, I think doing four things during COVID-19 saved me: Going through Coro Women in Leadership, restarting Decorating Details, starting a live cooking show, and attending Duquesne University to earn my professional coaching certificate. This is how I chose to empower myself, and it's proof that you can do the same. Believe in what you can do while you pivot and step into your success. And remember, there does not have to be a global pandemic to make changes and shifts in your life.

How will you pivot and shift into new success all while empowering your future? It is out there waiting for you; just do it.

This is dedicated to my friend Ray Kaluzny. He taught me everything I know about drapery, and then some. I am a success because of him.

Bio

Photo by Ryan Farrow

Renee DeMichiei-Farrow is an entrepreneur, small business advocate, and author who is highly lauded for business branding, marketing, business development, public relations, government relations, and coaching.

Renee founded the award-winning custom window treatment business Decorating Details, LLC in 1992 and has relaunched it in 2020! In her full-time work, she is director of business development for a woman-owned architectural firm in Pittsburgh.

She was honored as a 2015 Plum High School Distinguished Alumni and started a scholarship for the TV production students in memory of her parents, with the help of her three brothers. Renee's long list of awards, in short, also includes Athena Finalist and PA Best 50 Women in Business.

Known for her civic commitment, Renee currently serves on the boards of Gwen's Girls (as vice-chair) and South Western PA Engineers Organization. She is also part of the United Way Women's Leadership Council. Renee is a graduate of Leadership Pittsburgh XIX, Coro Women in Leadership and has her professional coaching certification from Duquesne University.

Renee will tell everyone and anyone who will listen: Her biggest accomplishment is her family. Married to retired City of Pittsburgh EMS Chief Bob Farrow for 43 years, they have raised three successful children—Rob, Rachel, and Ryan—and they are the doting and loving grandparents of two beautiful grandchildren—Jack Andrew and Ellie An.

Connect with Renee

LinkedIn: www.linkedin.com/in/reneedemichieifarrow

Twitter: @demichieifarrow

Facebook: www.facebook.com/reneedemichieifarrow
www.facebook.com/cookingwithreneedemichieifarrow

Website: www.decorating-details.com

Coaching with Renee: renee@resultswithreneefarrow.coach

Giving Back: I will offer you a free 30-minute coaching session!

Empower Book: Email Renee at rf@decorating-details.com
$12.50 includes shipping

Ditch Drama and Take Charge of Your Story

Merilee Smith

Cheers to you for choosing the entrepreneur adventure, and welcome to the club! It's a life full of freedom, daring leaps, never-ending personal growth, and endless possibilities.

I've personally been a member of this club since 2009 with no regrets! Has my story been smooth-sailing without challenges, fears, bumps, and the year 2020? LOL, of course not! This would be a pretty damn boring chapter if that were the case.

My goal is to share with you not only my lessons learned, but, more importantly, the key superpower to being an incredibly successful business owner! Exciting, right? But I'm getting ahead of myself. First, allow me to introduce myself . . .

My name is Merilee Smith, and I'm a drama disruptor and life empowerment coach. When I share this elevator pitch with new acquaintances, the eager response is always, "You had me at drama disruptor." Then it's followed with a puzzled look and the question, "But what exactly does this mean?"

If you've ever doubted yourself, been frustrated, or felt overwhelmed, you've experienced drama.

If you've been procrastinating going after your dreams, you're in drama.

And let's not forget about those days when you look in the mirror and say, "Who do you think you are? What makes you think you've got what it takes to be your own boss and bring in the dough?" BINGO . . . that's drama!

Before I go further, if you've experienced any of the above—and I suspect you have—please know you are completely and utterly normal. It's part of the entrepreneurial roller coaster ride. Give yourself some space and grace.

To put a finer point on it, this is drama of the worst kind because it's inner drama. It's you being in battle with your thoughts, beliefs, and emotions. At least when you're in conflict with another person, you can walk away. With inner drama, you are trapped in your own mind. It can suck your energy and feast on your self-worth and confidence.

I'm also a guru on such drama because I know it intimately. As an entrepreneur, my sabotaging thoughts and beliefs kept me in Stucksville far too long—I mean, for years. Zoinks! The fabulous news is that there is indeed a way to ditch this drama and come out the champion! I've discovered this superpower. It's precisely why I've dedicated my work to helping others transform their drama so they can live to their potential—a happy and abundant life full of passion and purpose.

So, What's the Power?

If you want to be ALL IN on your business, then you absolutely must be willing to get up close and personal with your thoughts, beliefs, and emotions and understand how they impact your life. Because, I promise you, they are driving your daily actions and decisions and creating your future. Your positive thoughts will spark the empowering energy you need to keep moving forward, no matter what. And in a nanosecond, negative beliefs, such as fear or doubt, can paralyze you. To sum this up, your thoughts and emotions are the powerhouses to your success. Learning to master your mind is a non-negotiable skill for a committed entrepreneur.

Allow me to bring this to life by sharing my drama-to-empowerment story and my quest to becoming a life coach.

My Journey from Drama to Empowerment

I've always believed that happiness is the key to life and that we all deserve this. My heart believed this so much that I went to work for Walt Disney World—the place where happiness and dreams come true. As a people leader for Disney, I was truly energized to bring out the best in others. I loved this so much that I obtained my master's degree in the field of people and organizational development.

From here, I worked for a prominent leadership development company, facilitating corporate leadership development programs across an array of industries. While this role was fulfilling, I knew something was missing. As I grew up working in my parents' community pharmacy, I realized I also had this entrepreneurial fire within me and that I wanted to help others and be the master of my destiny.

In 2009, I quit my full-time training job and became an independent contractor. I still facilitated corporate training programs but at my own will. This gave me the opportunity to start my own consulting business. My mission was to help smaller businesses build healthy work cultures where people felt valued, empowered, and engaged while also having opportunities to grow.

This decision gave me the freedom to go after my dream. And yet, I didn't feel free or empowered. In fact, I felt quite the opposite. I knew I wanted my consulting business to take off, but I felt lost and didn't know where to start. At first, I thought I had the answer. I hired a business coach to help me put a solid strategy in place. After thousands of dollars, and six months later, I walked away with good ideas on how I could move my business forward. But my biggest insight was that I had a crap load of limiting beliefs and confidence issues to deal with if I were to ever make it as an entrepreneur.

Since I have been living in the self-help section for years, I figured the mindset stuff would naturally come, so I put it on the backburner. My priority was to keep pushing forward on my goals of serving my existing clients and getting new ones. But my actions told another story. I continued to hang on to my corporate contract position because it was the easy road. It gave me a good income while allowing me to teach others and travel to cool places. As long as I kept this gig going, I was golden! I would never have to deal with my fears of going ALL IN on my own business. I could stay safe and comfy without risk.

Here's the truth about ignoring your fears: They never go away; they go deeper. As time went on, I became increasingly dissatisfied with my work and, even worse, with myself. I knew I was settling for mediocrity and that I wasn't being true to myself. I felt crappy for surrendering my dreams to my insecurities. This only caused my confidence to plummet more. And I took my misery out on those I loved most, draining their energy. I was caught in a vicious cycle of inner drama.

Because I had already studied the concept of emotional awareness and gained insight about the importance of mindset, I was able to recognize that my thoughts and emotions were keeping me stuck. I was exhausted from hating myself. These feelings certainly were not serving me nor my goals. I knew I needed help at a deeper level and decided to hire another coach. Only this time, I hired a mindset coach to help me conquer and transform my doubts once and for all. As a result, I was able to liberate myself from my negative beliefs—and I haven't looked back.

Fast forward to 2020 . . .

With a free mind, my intuition kicked in. I gained an insane amount of clarity in my business. Just before COVID hit the United States, I realized that my heart was no longer with business consulting. My true desire is to help people be happy in all areas of their life, not just at work. After 11 years, I quit my contract income, and I said YES to reinventing myself as a life coach in 2020 and being ALL IN on my business!

It was like I flipped a switch in my head. I felt completely empowered and owned my identity as a CEO. I trusted myself and my mission with conviction. I wasted no time building my new brand on social media as a life coach and thought leader.

Old me was terrified to post my thoughts, but the new me played full out. I started my own Facebook community and dove right in doing live videos to connect with my audience. I wanted to shine my talents so others would know how I can help them live their best lives. In today's virtual world it's vital to have a consistent online presence. People do business with people they know, like, and trust, with those they see value in.

I started my LLC, Coach With Merilee, and created a new logo. This was an extremely energizing experience. Every time I see my logo, my heart screams, "This is me!" You know you're on the right path when you can feel it in your soul.

I also tapped into my training and development expertise and created a robust coaching program that allows my clients to achieve life-changing results. It's important to note that our skills and experiences are never wasted; they are an intentional part of our journey that will serve their purpose at the right times.

I re-engaged with my former business coach because guess what! This time I was mentally and emotionally prepared to focus on growing my business. I learned a simple yet powerful marketing strategy to attract my ideal clients, and before I knew it, I signed my first client and then some more. It's onward and upward from here!

2020 will indeed go down in the history books. For me, it will be the red-letter year that I believed in myself with my full heart and became the resourceful, resilient CEO of my business and life.

Your Thoughts and Emotions Are Everything

The biggest wisdom I can emphasize for you is that your thoughts and emotions are everything! Please do not underestimate them.

They've been forming in your subconscious throughout your life based on your experiences and the things people and society have told you. Your thoughts create your identity and what you believe about yourself. They will either help you or significantly limit you in life. If you want to stay in the game, you must believe in who you are as an entrepreneur and in what you do with unwavering faith.

My story is a perfect example of this. Because of my past stories and old beliefs, I told myself that I was neither smart nor good enough to run my own business. As a result, I resided in fear and in Stucksville. I'm grateful to the powers above that I gained the awareness and emotional agility to handle my emotions and upgrade my beliefs. It's scary to think about where I would be if I hadn't—perhaps I would be the mayor of Stucksville.

Twenty Won

If you're struggling with your business, it's a safe bet there's some internal garbage going on in your head that you need to manage and clear. Again, these feelings are normal, especially when you're moving beyond your comfort zone. Please don't lose heart. Building your emotional agility will help you tame these inner demons. This means embracing ALL of your emotions, both the positive and negative ones. Your emotions are your best friends. They are constantly telling you when something in your life is aligned and going well and when it isn't. They tell you when you are showing up as your best, empowered self in your biz or when you're caught in drama. Remember drama can paralyze you.

When you're aware of your thoughts and how they drive your emotions and decisions, you become the jedi master of your mind. You become open, creative, and agile to whatever comes your way. My emotions and thoughts are my true north. Emotional agility is the number one superpower of a business owner. It's what guides me every day. It's what helped me persevere in 2020 and come out stronger on the other side.

As a fellow entrepreneur, I'm loudly cheering you on! You've got this, and I'm proud to be your colleague!

The last thing I will say is this . . . Knowing you have inner drama is one thing, but ditching it is another. Often, we're too close to our own story to see what is really going on at the core. Please don't wait, like I did, to get help. Asking for help is a strength. I highly encourage you to hire a coach ASAP. He or she will be your thinking partner, support, and confidant.

Getting in the right mindset will make all the difference. It will accelerate your growth and success exponentially! Remember, you must do the inner work before the outer will work. Master your mind, and you will always have the power to take charge of your story!

Bio

Photo by Dominique Murray

Merilee is a high-energy life coach and drama disruptor who is extremely passionate about helping people get off autopilot and reconnect with their authentic self. She helps her clients ignite their inner power so they can take charge of their story and live a life full of purpose and passion.

Once we hit a certain age, we awake to discover that we've been just going through the motions of life. We lose sight of what's really important to us. We often feel disconnected or lost. We start to question who we are and what we really want out of life. As Ferris Bueller so eloquently states, "Life moves pretty fast. If you don't stop and look around once in a while, you could miss it." Merilee makes sure her clients don't miss it!

As a thinking partner, she helps her clients claim their happiness by getting clear on what they deeply want for themselves, in their relationships, and career. She helps disrupt any internal drama such as negative beliefs holding them back. With over 20 years of experience facilitating and coaching in the leadership and people development space,

Merilee gives her clients the empowerment and emotional tools they need to live their best life.

Connect with Merilee

Being a member of the entrepreneurs' club allows you to expand your network with the most energizing, inspiring, and supportive group of colleagues you could ever imagine. This book is an excellent example of this.

I'd love to connect. You can find me at the following:

Website: www.coachwithmerilee.com

LinkedIn: www.linkedin.com/in/merilee-smith-coachwithmerilee/

Facebook Community: www.facebook.com/groups/claimyourhappiness

Instagram: www.instagram.com/coachwithmerilee/

This is NOT What I Expected!

Gloria Ward

"Gloria, we have to refund everyone their money! We can't do the event! This coronavirus is getting bad," my publicist said disappointedly from the other side of the phone. "Six months of work down the drain," she said. I asked her to wait a little to see if things would slow down, but it only ended up getting worse. People everywhere were panicking, and every time you turned on the news, it showed just how rapidly the virus was spreading.

A couple of days later, I told my publicist to cancel the launch for our coaching program for women. The event was to be our coming-out party to introduce us to the masses. We had spent money on plane tickets, hotels, event space, and everything else you can think of, most of which was non-refundable.

"Do you think this virus is going to impact your business?" my publicist asked. "I hope not," I answered. "I'm hoping we can get through this and just postpone until the spring." As time went on, however, we started seeing people wearing masks, getting sick, and even dying. No one knew what this virus was and surely didn't know how to contain it. We started relying heavily on social media to keep in contact with our members and constantly giving them updates on events.

The more I watched the news and read the blogs, the more I started feeling like we might have to pivot. The government was talking about a nationwide lockdown which would kill our business. While we normally relied on workshops, events, and seminars to interact with our women and sell our products and services, now we would have to find creative ways to connect and stay connected.

For the first couple of days, I had no ideas. Our business was new but not unique. We were only two years old and did not have the branding or the reputation to coast through a lockdown. I scheduled a meeting with my team so we could brainstorm some ideas. After two hours, we asked ourselves one question, "What can we do to continue to help our women with their personal growth while in a pandemic?" The answer we decided on was SERVE.

On the brink of a nationwide lockdown, we knew our women would essentially be confined to their homes. Furthermore, we knew that some of those women would not be in the best situations while at home. Some would be alone, some home with their abusers, and some with their children trying to figure out how to manage the household. Most of them would lose their jobs based on their occupation. If they were frontline workers, they were working all the time. If not, they were working virtually or not at all.

With such a big change, we decided not to focus on ourselves but to crank up everything we were already doing and rely on technology to help us get it done. Since I had a background in Information Technology, I was able to reach out to some of my tech friends for advice. Social media was our biggest tool. Most, if not all, of our members and potential members were on Facebook, which we used to talk to our members and give them an encouraging word.

The more the pandemic and lockdown became a reality, the more we served. We started going live every day, inspiring and motivating any woman who would listen, interviewing experts on the virus to help our women understand how to protect themselves and their households. We knew that, if we could get our women in a space where they could continue their personal growth journey and laugh, we were doing our job.

While social media was important, we also experienced a setback. My Facebook account got hacked, and I lost my profile, meaning I no longer had access to my business and personal pages. I panicked so badly because we worked hard to let our members know to join us there for updates and information. Our business page survived because a team member set it up with their account. Whew, I thought. If we would have lost that page, our whole business would've been gone.

After weeks of trying to get my profile back with Facebook, I had no success. That experience taught me a great lesson. Never ever have your audience on one platform that you do not control. I realized that the social media gods could take away my business anytime they wanted, and I could not let that happen. We started asking everyone on social media to join our mailing list, which we now keep two copies of: one on my external drive and the other on our mailing-list software, which grows and shrinks every day.

We also started holding our events virtually. At first, the interaction was not the same. People were forgetting the times, stayed for 10 minutes and left, didn't turn their cameras on, or just didn't participate. In person, we are able to point out those who are shy and help them loosen up, but online, we had no control of their environment or their time.

We realized that our women wanted to participate in the sessions, but they were suffering from virtual-meeting fatigue. They were on virtual meetings for work, meetings, and even for parent- teacher conversations. If it wasn't something that interested them in the first 10 minutes, they would log off.

To get around this, we started doing on-demand sessions. We didn't want our women to feel like they were stuck to a specific date and time, so we allowed them to experience the workshop, seminar, or livestream whenever they were ready. When they did finally watch, we would get a notification, and one of our team members would follow up. This was much more effective because our women watched during the quiet time at night or early in the morning before work.

Twenty Won

Aware that the lockdown was putting incredible stress and pressure on women seemingly everywhere, we wanted to make sure we were there when they needed us. We created a hotline where women could call to vent. If they were home alone and just needed someone to talk to, we were someone they could call. We ran ads on social media and received hundreds of calls a day. Women from around the nation were calling, letting us know how the pandemic had changed their lives for better or worse and how they had to wait in line just to get some toilet paper.

What this taught us is that, as we were serving, we were not only increasing our brand, but we had direct contact with our members and potential members to see what they wanted and what was important to them. Each week my team and I would reassess where we were and if we were doing the kind of service the women were looking for.

Financially, things were slow. Since money was tight, we could not charge our regular rates for our events, and sometimes we didn't charge at all. We had to make some adjustments in personnel, cut back on advertising, and shift from spending money to spending time. We made phone calls, answered messages, and even met people in person to help them understand what our business was and how we could help.

We did this throughout 2020, and we are so happy we did. We created so much connection with our women and received such great feedback, so much so that in 2021, we do not have to play the guessing game on what our women want. After all, they spent an entire year telling us.

Key Takeaways

1. Always assess where you are and pivot when necessary. The pandemic forced us to take a hard look at ourselves and our business. Most of us never really sit down and see if we are really growing or if we need to change. Assess your business once a month, and ask yourself if you're moving in the right direction. If you find that the answer is no, then you might want to think about pivoting.

2. Get with your team. There is an African proverb that says, "If you want to go fast, go alone. If you want to go far, go together." Building a team is a surefire way to help you achieve your goals and business success. Your team will help you see things that you can't see and give you ideas that you've never thought of. Your team is closest to the people, so listening to them and getting ideas is vital to how far you go.

3. Become a problem solver. So many things have and went wrong in 2020. People have lost their jobs or even died. If you didn't know how to problem solve before, you learned how throughout the pandemic. As business owners, we have to remember that problems are predictors as well as reminders. In every problem, there is an opportunity, and each is solvable. If your business didn't survive or you had to put it on hold, go back and revisit what the problem was and see how you can turn it around now that you have a fresh start.

4. Never be satisfied. Never be satisfied with where you are. Always test, fail, learn, improve, and get back to work. Having a never-satisfied attitude will help you keep going when everything else around you seems to

be crumbling. Let me be clear—I'm not saying to keep trying things that are not working. What I'm saying is, if you went through the process of testing, failing, learning, and improving, and it's still not working out, don't quit. Find another way to get it done. Don't settle.

5. Practice Self-Discipline. *New York Times* bestselling author, coach, and speaker John Maxwell says, "Everything worthwhile is uphill." You have to climb the ladder of success every day. Self-discipline is the difference between temporary success and sustainable success. If you want a business that will be around for years to come, the bridge to getting there is self-discipline. Make sure you're doing something every day that's moving you closer to your goals. Remember, there's nothing you can do to make an undisciplined person successful. If you have some goals and dreams you want to achieve, with faith, action, and self-discipline, you will get there.

Bio

Gloria Ward is an entrepreneur, revenue strategist, author, and New Thought leader who has been at the forefront of helping women and women business owners learn, earn, advance, and profit.

She's the revenue strategist that small businesses turn to for guidance. For more than 12 years, clients have enjoyed the confidence, humor, and relatable step-by-step strategies of her business advice and tactics. Her company, The L.E.A.P. Group LLC, and viral movement, The I'm Loving Me Project, are personal development and business education branches that inspire and empower women to win the game of life and build a million-dollar business from scratch.

It was Gloria's passion for business and her down-to-earth approach that helped make her the most sought-out female entrepreneur of her era. Gloria is a big lover of music and lives in Atlanta, Ga., where she is a mom of two four-legged creatures.

Connect with Gloria

Website: www.imlovingme.net
Book: www.amazon.com/Becoming-Truly-You-healing-creating-ebook/

I'm Not Busy

Holly Joy McIlwain

"The events of 2020 have turned workplaces upside down. Under the highly challenging circumstances of the COVID-19 pandemic, many employees are struggling to do their jobs. Many feel like they're 'always on' now that the boundaries between work and home have blurred. They're worried about their family's health and finances. Burnout is a real issue. Women in particular have been negatively impacted. Women—especially women of color—are more likely to have been laid off or furloughed during the COVID-19 crisis, stalling their careers and jeopardizing their financial security1."

- Excerpt from the 2020 Women in the Workplace study.[1]

---

[1] www.mckinsey.com/featured-insights/diversity-and-inclusion/women-in-the-workplace

I am the founder of a high-impact nonprofit organization that aims to create a space for professional women to move into brave action. Starting a nonprofit in the midst of a pandemic is a direct response to the experiences that too many professional women are working through. We provide a space for women to receive unprecedented support during this pivotal moment in history, under our motto, "Do Brave Things." This started with how the last couple of years started to unfold for me.

On a Tuesday morning in 2019, the owner of the firm invited me into the boardroom for a meeting. One of the partners was present. And I was being let go. With class and confusion, I packed up my office. Driving home, I secured my next role with Winner Partners, a retained-search firm that focused on people first. That was exactly what was needed. But generating revenue and building business was also needed. I began working immediately and took on the mantra, "Do one brave thing every day." This propelled me forward into not only building a strong professional reputation, but also completing my first book, accepting an additional position at an esteemed university, and barreling towards 40 with a few goals still left to achieve.

When 2020 hit, I wasn't terribly worried. My kids were home with me, safe and healthy. My work was secure. We were okay.

Over the next six months, my father-in-law discovered that he had stage 4 metastatic melanoma, which moved to his brain, lung, and colon, and he moved into our home; my husband was diagnosed with MS; and my own father passed away. No one is ever prepared for the death of a parent. There were many unresolved family issues during the time of my dad's passing which resulted in me suffering a miscarriage. We experienced more grief than any family ever deserved to, in such a short period of time. The trauma, pain, and shock nearly did me in. I needed to knit my own broken body and heart back together, as I was being held comfortingly and continuously, as if in a mother's arms, by a group of women who didn't even really know each other yet. We were championing my own Brave Women Project, and when I decided to take some time off for reconstructive surgery (with a little Mommy Makeover thrown in), we committed to building a place for others to be healed and supported as well.

The pandemic didn't impact my business, but life certainly did. In building and launching a high-impact nonprofit organization during such a tumultuous time, I harnessed the energy and bravery that my support system poured into me. We focus on delivering development and mentorship opportunities for women, which directly and positively impacts their physical and mental health, financial wellness, and professional and educational development, while building their network in non-traditional and virtual methods. We believe that the ability to move into brave action comes from our community of women as we experience the power of unparalleled encouragement. Through peer-to-peer education and constant evolution, we engage women as they identify areas in their lives where bravery is needed. We all know that those areas look and feel different for everyone, so I tapped into my own evolving needs and my encouraging network to build something that could meet women where they are and give them the guts to go where they want to go.

We build everything around five actions for everyday life: evolve, educate, encourage, engage, and empower. These actions build bravery internally and, when they incorporate others, externally as well. I wanted a platform for professional women to get the support they needed when they needed it, so we incorporated monthly wellness plans and at-home workout videos from a motivational and trained exercise physiologist; featured monthly professional development at lunch time (a "Come as You Are" conversation for members only); and hosted (what started it all) a Saturday morning virtual brunch. Every month we offer opportunities for women to connect, be seen, and receive the support that we all need. Let's be honest, many professional women do hard things every day. We work hard, make difficult decisions, and over half of us work the second shift at home as caretakers. If we are going to carve out time to get support, it has to be in small doses and convenient. Our Brave Women Project does just that. And we are already changing lives.

But how did it happen? I have two high-intensity careers already. A mom of two small boys, I care about wellness, spirituality, and harmony in my life. I wasn't willing to dive into starting another venture if any of these things would be jeopardized, and I realized that there were a few things that had to be put in place for me personally before a project like this would be possible. As part of my commitment to "un-busy" habits and clearly established boundaries, I needed to be smart about my work. Maintaining a clear distinction, my time at work is purposeful, and my time with family is precious. I guard both with fervor and constantly have to evaluate priorities. I do this in a couple of ways:

Twenty Won

I act in a way that demonstrates the value of time—your time is no more or less important than my time. I use a calendar for everything and evaluate on Sunday evenings (with my husband) what's coming in the week ahead. We try to mitigate the risks of curveballs hitting us where the Good Lord split us.

Saying "no" is sometimes the kindest thing that I can do. There's something brave about saying "no" when we feel that we should say "yes," whether it's to the things that we really want or dread. And, I know for myself, harnessing that energy early on saves me the emotional and physical output that can be draining. In order to say "no" properly, I have to evaluate my own values and commitments. When I was a teenager attending endless chastity talks, we were taught that "No is a complete sentence." Well, if you're a people pleaser or a compulsive volunteer, it isn't that easy. Get yourself a few key phrases that you practice responding with so that you can buy time to evaluate and contemplate. Try one of these:

I will need to check with PARTNER and get back to you.

My calendar has been a little full lately; can you circle back to me at a later date so that I can focus my energy on this?

I'd like to support this, but I can't help at this time.

When do you need an answer? I'd like to think about it.

Chances are, there are people out there whose lives intersect with your life pretty intimately, whether they be life or business partners. For those people, communication is everything. What works best in these relationships? Three things: 1) Mutual respect; 2) Shared goals and priorities; and 3) Communication. In fact, do this: Overcommunicate. Overcommunicate. Overcommunicate.

I know this may be hard to believe, but one of the best things I've ever done was being brave enough to start the Brave Women Project in the midst of everything else that I do. I benefit directly from the support, professional development, and challenge to be my authentic self. I've learned that I do not have to do it all, that creativity and play are absolutely necessary, and that everyone needs room to be un-busy.

Bio

Photo by Jordan Louise Photography

Holly Joy McIlwain is the founder and chief cheerleader of the Brave Women Project. She is the author of *For She Who Leads: Practical Wisdom from a Woman Who Serves* and leads the talent development platform at Winner Partners.

Holly is a subject-matter expert in the usage of behavior assessments as part of coaching and development plans. As a Gallup Certified Strengths Coach, Holly has a passion for building a better world through sustainable business solutions, while her professional purpose is developing leaders who change lives.

Holly holds an advanced degree in organizational leadership from Robert Morris University and is certified as a DISC behavior analyst and a Driving Forces Behavior Analyst. Holly serves as faculty for Pittsburgh Leadership Foundation and is a DDI certified facilitator. An expert in the value of dynamic onboarding as part of the foundation for fully engaged employees, Holly is the human resources business partner for talent management at Robert Morris University and seeks new ways to challenge leaders to become fully engaged in transformation. What's not exciting about that?

Holly brings this enthusiasm with her into each coaching session, team workshop, search opportunity, and speaking engagement, and it carries right over into the Brave Women Project. Nothing excites Holly more than inspiring women to do brave things.

She and her husband, Kevin, are raising two young boys and residing in the Greater Pittsburgh, Pa., area.

Connect with Holly

www.BWP.life
Instagram @bravewomenproject

Conclusion

THANK YOU to the other 20 women who shared their stories with us. I'm not sure if I'll ever be able to put into words how much this project means to me and how incredible each of these women made me feel when they said "Yes" to participating. I have not only learned a lot about myself, but a lot about them, and I will be forever grateful for every moment spent creating this publication. We have a bond that will be cherished for many, many years to come. I can only hope I lived up to their expectations and that they reflect on this journey with unlimited excitement and pride forever.

To say something along the lines of, "I hope you enjoyed this book," doesn't nearly speak to the impact I hope these stories have on you. There are so many inspiring (the word "inspiration" was used 17 times) stories of strong (24 times) women who pivoted (23 times) to make their dreams come true, in what was a year for the record books—2020.

I must ask, "What did you learn?" If you're a female entrepreneur who's been in business for years, if you're just starting out, or if you are putting ideas together to start a business, there are lessons within these pages. Who did you resonate with the most? Was it on a personal or professional level—or both? I encourage you to connect with one, two, or all the contributors. Lean on us for support ("support" was used a whopping 66 times!) and strength (14 times). Take full advantage of connecting with us on our social media outlets. Send an email letting us know how you feel about this book and how it has helped you. Share your thoughts with us. Knowing these ladies, I can tell you each message will be thoughtfully read and appreciated!

Thank you, dear reader, for choosing this book and making 21 women incredibly happy and proud!

As I close, I need to recognize a few people. A very special thank you goes out to my writing coach and editor, Cori Wamsley, and her team; to Mj Callaway for all the above-and-beyond support and time she invested in this project; to Karen Captline for her patience and "informal therapy" while creating what would become the beautiful cover to this book; to Melanie Colusci and her Mastermind group—for connecting me with so many of the contributing authors; and to Renee DeMichiei Farrow for giving me the push I needed to make this dream come true. Renee, I will cherish your guidance and friendship forever. Thank you to my husband, Rob, for always believing in me and allowing me the creative freedom to be happy; to my kids, Cameron (and Kirstyn) and Kayla (and Zach), for being people I am proud of every single day; to my sister, Jaime (I wish dad was here to see this!), for pushing me to get outside and walk during these long winter months—even when it was 20 degrees, and I was too busy and too tired; to my extended family and friends for their interest and enthusiasm; and to my mom, Candice. It's true when they say . . . your mom will always be your number one fan.

~ Kelli A. Komondor

Made in the USA
Columbia, SC
27 April 2021